Feisty Fragments
For Philosophy

Feisty Fragments
For Philosophy
Vincent F. Hendricks

© Individual author and King's College 2004. All rights reserved.

ISBN 1-904-987-01-X
King's College Publications
Scientific Director: Dov Gabbay
Managing Director: Jane Spurr
Department of Computer Science
Strand, London WC2R 2LS, UK
kcp@dcs.kcl.ac.uk

Cover design by Richard Fraser, www.avalonarts.co.uk
Printed by Lightning Source, Milton Keynes, UK

All rights reserved. No part of this publication may be reproduced, stored in a retrieval system or transmitted, in any form, or by any means, electronic, mechanical, photocopying, recording or otherwise, without prior permission, in writing, from the publisher.

To the freaks

Milton Walther Hendricks

and

Lucy Saturna Fry

Contents

Preface	xi
Disclaimer	xv

1 A   1
- Douglas Adams 1
- Henry Brooks Adams 1
- John Adams 2
- Louisa May Alcott 2
- † Anonymous 2
- Isaac Asimov 5
- Alfred J. Ayer 6
- William E. Aytoun 6

2 B   7
- Francis Bacon 7
- Roger Bacon 8
- Walter Bagehot 8
- Mikhail A. Bakunin 9
- Renford Bambrough 9
- George Bataille 9
- Henry Ward Beecher 10
- Ludwig van Beethoven 10
- Jeremy Bentham 10
- Nicolas Berdyaev 11
- John Berger 11
- Henri Bergson 11
- George Berkeley 12
- Isaiah Berlin 12

Ambrose Bierce 13
Antoinette Brown Blackwell 14
Marguerite Blessington 15
Ned Block 15
Niels Bohr 15
Edward de Bono 16
Daniel J. Boorstin 16
Marx Born 16
James Boswell 17
Francis Herbert Bradley 17
Mel Brooks 18
Joyce Brothers 18
Charlie Brown 18
Thomas Browne 19
Giordano Bruno 19
Edward Bulwer-Lytton 20
Vannevar Bush 20
Samuel Butler 20

3 C **23**

Thomas Campbell 23
Albert Camus 23
Elias Canetti 24
Thomas Carlyle 24
Rudolf Carnap 24
Rachel Carson 25
Sebastian-Roch-Nicholas Chamfort 25
Alexander Chase 26
John Cheever 26
G.K. Chesterton 26
Marcus Tullius Cicero 27
Arthur C. Clarke 28
Samuel T. Coleridge 28
John Churton Collins 28
Anne Finch Conway 29
Mason Cooley 29
Libby Copeland 29
Victor Cousin 30
Stephen Crane 30
David Cronenberg 30

4 D — 31
- Jean D'Alembert 31
- Daniel C. Dennett 31
- René Descartes 32
- John Dewey 33
- Denis Diderot 34
- Diogenes [the Cynic] 34
- Michele Le Doeuff 35
- Lord Dunsany 35
- Ariel Durant 36
- Will Durant 36

5 E — 37
- Oliver Edwards 37
- Paul Edwards 37
- Albert Einstein 38
- George Eliot 39
- Thomas Stearns Eliot 39
- Hugh Elliot 40
- Ralph Waldo Emerson 40
- Epictetus 41
- Nominis Expers 42

6 F — 43
- Ludwig Feurbach 43
- Paul Feyerabend 43
- Richard P. Feynman 44
- Melvin Fitting 45
- Anthony Flew 45
- Jerry Fodor 46
- La Bovier de Fontenelle 46
- Benjamin Franklin 47
- Gottlob Frege 47
- James A. Froude 47

7 G — 49
- John Kenneth Galbraith 49
- Galileo Galilei 49
- John W. Gardner 50
- José Ortega y Gassett 50

Paul Gauguin 51
Ernest Gellner 51
William E. Gladstone 51
Kahlil Gibran 52
Clark Glymour 52
Nelson Goodman 53
Johan Wolfgang von Goethe 53
Oliver Goldsmith 53
Rebecca Goldstein 54
Catherine the Great 54
Phillip Guedalla 54

8 H   **55**
Ian Hacking 55
William Hamilton 56
D.W. Hamlyn 56
Christopher Hampton 56
Sydney J. Harris 57
Stephen W. Hawking 57
William Hazlitt 58
William Randolph Hearst 58
Heathiana 58
Georg Friedrich Hegel 59
Martin Heidegger 59
Piet Hein 60
Werner Heisenberg 60
John Herschel 61
Abraham Joshua Heschel 61
Jaakko Hintikka 61
Thomas Hobbes 62
Wilfrid Hodges 62
Oliver Wendell Holmes, Jr. 63
Ted Honderich 63
Elbert Hubbard 63
David Hume 64
Aldous Huxley 65
Thomas Huxley 65

9 I   **67**
Irish Philosophy of Life 67

10 J — 69
Karl Gustav Jacobi 69
William James 69
Samuel Johnson 71
Benjamin Jowett 71

11 K — 73
Horace Meyer Kallen 73
Immanuel Kant 73
John Keats 74
John F. Kennedy 74
Johannes Kepler 75
Charles F. Kettering 75
Dick Keyes 76
Søren Aabye Kierkegaard 76
Joseph Wood Krutch 77

12 L — 79
George Lakoff 79
Dalai Lama 79
Walter Savage Landor 80
Suzanne K. Langer 80
Timothy Leary 80
Henri Lebesgue 81
Emmanuel Levinas 81
George Henry Lewes 82
Clive Staples Lewis 82
Georg C. Lichtenberg 82
Walter Lippmann 83

13 M — 85
Thomas Babington Macaulay 85
J.L. Mackie 85
Michael Maier 86
Joseph De Maistre 86
Emma Martin 86
Karl Marx 87
W. Somerset Maugham 87
James Clerk Maxwell 87
Lou Marinoff 88

James McCosh 88
Peter Brian Medawar 89
H.L. Mencken 90
Mary Midgley 90
Robert A. Millikan 91
John Milton 91
Michel de Montaigne 91
Hans J. Morgenthau 92
Herbert J. Muller 92
Iris Murdoch 93

14 N 95
John Henry Newman 95
Isaac Newton 95
Friedrich Nietzsche 96
Novalis—Friedrich Freiherr von Hardenberg 97
Robert Nozick 98

15 O 99
Michael Oakeshott 99
Julius Robert Oppenheimer 99
Origen 100
P.D. Ouspensky 100

16 P 101
Philippus Aureolus Paracelsus 101
Cyril Northcote Parkinson 102
David Papineau 102
Blaise Pascal 102
Boris L. Pasternak 103
Charles Peguy 103
Charles S. Peirce 103
Albert Pike 104
Robert M. Pirsig 105
Max Planck 105
Plotinus 106
Plutarch 106
Henri Poincaré 107
Michael Polanyi 107
Terrence Pratchett 108

J.J. Procter 108
Hilary Putnam 109

17 Q   111
Queen Victoria 111
Willard v. Quine 111
Anthony Quinton 112

18 R   113
Frank Ramsey 113
Ayn Rand 113
W. Winwood Reade 114
Thomas Reid 114
Nicolas Rescher 115
Charles Richter 115
Francois De La Rochefoucauld 115
Jean Jacques Rousseau 116
Richard Rorty 116
Bertrand Russell 117
Gilbert Ryle 119

19 S   121
Marquis de Sade 121
Carl Sagan 121
Seigneur de Saint-Evremond 122
George Santayana 122
Jean Paul Sartre 123
Friedrich von Schlegel 123
Friedrich Schleirmacher 124
Arthur Schopenhauer 124
Charles Schulz 124
John Selden 125
William Shakespeare 125
George Bernard Shaw 126
J.J.C. Smart 126
Adam Smith 127
George H. Smith 127
Raymond M. Smullyan 127
Socrates 128
Herbert Spencer 128

CONTENTS

Oswald Spengler 128
Vilhjálmur Stefánsson 129
Gertrude Stein 129
James Stephens 130
Wallace Stevens 130
Tom Stoppard 130
Harriet Beecher Stowe 131
P.F. Strawson 131
August Strindberg 131
Adam Swift 132

20 T 133
Charles Taylor 133
Alfred Lord Tennyson 133
James Thomson 134
Henry David Thoreau 134
W.H. Thorpe 135
James Thurber 135
Lev Nikolaevich Tolstoi 136
Mark Twain 136

21 V 137
Stephen Vizinczey 137
Francois Marie Arouet Voltaire 137
Bernard de Voto 138

22 W 139
Frans de Waal 139
Mary Warnock 139
Kevin Warwick 140
Alan W. Watts 140
Simone Weil 141
Steven Weinberg 141
Tom Weller 142
Alfred N. Whitehead 142
Norbert Wiener 143
P. Eugene Wigner 144
Oscar Wilde 144
Thornton Wilder 145
Edward O. Wilson 145

Ludwig Wittgenstein 145
William Wordsworth 147

23 Z   **149**
Robert Zend 149

Bibliography   **150**

Acknowledgements   **173**

Index   **180**

Preface

The alchemists of the Middle Ages searched for what is known as *lapis philosophorum* or the philosophers' stone. It was believed to be the stuff that could turn simple metals into gold and cure the most virulent diseases. Alchemists called themselves philosophers but were looked upon as magicians and wizards. Today there are no Alchemists. But there still exists a cadre of thinkers who look for a turn of phrase, a way of viewing the world. They allegedly turn the understanding of the experience of life into pure gold.

Academic philosophers have always had a way of obscuring the admirable endeavour of philosophy. This is emphasized by suggesting rather odd and exotic prerequisites for solving a seemingly simple problem; a particular jargon in which no words occurring have less than seven syllables. Outrageous thought experiments ask you to consider the situation in which evil demons are determined to fool you into believing that you are driving by a real barn when in fact it is made out of papermaché; or imagine your brain separated from the rest of your body floating around in a vat of nutritious fluids. Suppose there are other worlds than the one we know of in which you have a counterpart looking exactly like you and in which a most familiar thing like water has absolutely nothing to do with water!

The list of 'respectable' science fiction stories goes on and on and such thought experiments are really taken seriously in established academic philosophy—perhaps more now than ever before for some strange reason. When you pair up the impenetrable jargon with ludicrous thought experiments and continue to seriously insist that you are addressing the fundamental problems of the human existence and condition, it begins to sound pretty much like medieval alchemy to me—and apparently to a host of other mortals. This is what *Feisty Fragments — For Philosophy* echoes in words from Nietzsche to Einstein, from Catherine the Great to John F. Kennedy.

How could you possibly get so much extra mileage out of philosophy? As far as I can see there is a reason dating back to the distinguished Greek philosophers Plato and especially Aristotle. Plato held the view that philosophers should rule the world since they were the most enlightened of mankind. Aristotle believed that philosophy, *theoria* as he called it, was the mother of all sciences. *Theoria* is the ultimate stage of knowledge, insight and shrewdness to which all and everybody should aspire. Ruling the world and the idea of *theoria* seem to have suited the vanity of philosophers and philosophical thinking for almost two millennia—with some exceptions.

The term 'philosophy' simply means passion for wisdom or love of knowledge. Wanting knowledge and wisdom is not a particularly philosophical thing. It is not only the business of philosophy, and philosophy is definitely not just the province of academic philosophers. We all inquire and ask questions because it is dispositional, it's in our blood as human beings. On a daily basis we wonder and encounter philosophical problems—big ones as well as small ones: What is this thing called existence? How is the cosmos built up? What is morally good? Why did I like the painting in the museum? Can the death penalty be justified, etc? We usually don't treat these problems in a way academic philosophy would. Instead, poems, novels and short stories are written, science fiction films are produced, sonatas are composed, scientific results are achieved and we discuss politics at a dinner party. This does not make the daily matters we consider less philosophical—they are the quintessential questions of philosophy. Thus philosophical problems concern us all, and from this perspective we're all well worthy of being called philosophers.

Feisty Fragments mirrors these points convincingly. That's the beauty of good quotations; they are units of thought or discourse with expressive power way beyond carefully thought out arguments, demonstrations or proofs.

There is a bonus too—a good laugh. Many of the quotations include an exquisite sense of humor, sometimes subtle, sometimes quite blunt like Joy Larkin Luca's:

> *There will be absolutely no sex in philosophy without philosophy getting knocked up by the sciences.*

And in the end, rightly or wrongly, what would philosophy be and where would philosophers be – *where would we all be* – without a good laugh?

———————————— Φ ————————————

I would like to thank a number of people for providing me with relevant material that I was unaware of. In particular my colleagues Aksel Haaning and Jens Høyrup have pointed me to interesting bits and pieces. Pelle Guldborg Hansen, likewise from my department, kindly assisted me in tracking down copyright holders and helped me immensely with the permissions logistics. And as always, my colleague, teacher and most trusted friend, Stig Andur Pedersen, is always there to encourage, to support, to supply and to enjoy subtle – and sometimes not too subtle – humor. My father, Elbert L. Hendricks also dropped valuable bits, pieces, fragments and is also always there when support and encouragement is needed.

My New York City family, including Mimi, Bent, Zara and Vianna Vang Olsen, has taught me what a good laugh is all about. I'm always grateful to Mimi and on this particular occassion I would like to thank her for providing many valuable suggestions for improving the preface.

I would like to thank all the publishers, literary agents and executors, copyright holders, permissions- and rights-executives for allowing me to quote the material used in *Feisty Fragments*. A separate detailed Acknowledgements section is provided by the end of the book.

I would like to thank my proof-reader Henriette 'Henry' Holm for catching many errors and mistakes.

Finally, I would like to extend my gratitude to King's College Publications, and in particular Scientific Director Prof. Dov

M. Gabbay for taking on this project, and to Managing Director Jane Spurr, and Editorial Assistant Anna Maros who have been extremely helpful during the final stages of preparation and publication.

—Vincent F. Hendricks
October 2004
London

Disclaimer

Material for *Feisty Fragments — For Philosophy* has been taken from all over; books, articles, tv- and radio-shows, the internet etc. Texts have sometimes been corrupt and references have been missing but all possible attempts have been made to reconstruct and track down as much and as many as possible and seek permission to quote. Where references are missing, the quotes may be considered attributed. Full apologies are granted for any errors and omissions. There are instances where it have been impossible to trace the copyright holders. If notified of any error or omission it will be rectified at the earliest opportunity.

The copyright holders who have explicitly requested a particular credit line immediately after the quoted material have been honored, but otherwise credits are to be found in the Bibliography and Acknowledgements sections.

—Vincent F. Hendricks
October 2004
London

1 A

Douglas Adams

⊢ 1952—2001 *English author*

There is a theory which states that if ever anyone discovers exactly what the Universe is for and why it is here, it will instantly disappear and be replaced by something even more bizarre and inexplicable. There is another theory which states that this has already happened. —[2]

Henry Brooks Adams

⊢ 1838—1918 *American globetrotter*

Philosophy: unintelligible answers to insoluble problems. —[1]: Ch. 24 (§ 26)

John Adams

⊢ 1767—1848 *American president*

I must study politics and war so that my sons may have liberty to study mathematics and philosophy. My sons ought to study mathematics and philosophy, geography, natural history, naval architecture, navigation, commerce and agriculture in order to give their children a right to study painting, poetry, music, architecture, statuary, tapestry, and porcelain. —[3]

Louisa May Alcott

⊢ 1832—1888 *American author*

My definition [of a philosopher] is of a man up in a balloon, with his family and friends holding the ropes which confine him to earth and trying to haul him down. —[241]

† Anonymous

Vain is the word of a philosopher which does not heal any suffering of man.

[On metaphysics] Much wrangling in things needless to be known.

[On the philosopher] One who always knows what to do until it happens to him.

[On a philosopher] One you never go to for advice.

[On philosophy] An individual's way of seeing the total thrust and pressure of the universe.

[On philosophy] Like a pigeon, something to admire as long as it isn't over your head.

Philosophy is a game with objectives and no rules. Mathematics is a game with rules and no objectives.

Religion is a man using a divining rod. Philosophy is a man using a pick and shovel.

A Chinese philosopher once had a dream that he was a butterfly. From that day on, he was never quite certain that he was not a butterfly, dreaming that he was a man.

Referee's report: This paper contains much that is new and much that is true. Unfortunately, that which is true is not new and that which is new is not true.

The philosophy exam was a piece of cake—which was a bit of a surprise, actually, because I was expecting some questions on a sheet of paper.

[On philosophy] The art of lying about the art of living.

What if there were no such thing as a hypothetical situation?

Your argument is sound ... nothing *but* sound.

There is no expedient to which a man will not go to avoid the real labor of thinking.

Philosophy: The search for non-existing answers to non-existing questions.

Philosopher: A blind man in a dark room looking for a black hat which is not there.

Philosophy is like the tower of Babel—everyone has a different understanding of the words they're speaking, so truth (like Babel's heaven) can never be reached.

I'm kind of tired ... I was up all night trying to round off infinity.

You will have an intellectual discussion with a potato, today. You'll be so caught up in whether it was Descartes or Voltaire who first advocated empiricism, that it will fail to strike you as a bit odd that the potato knows much of anything about 17th-century French philosophers. In fact, it knows more about them than you do. Later, that will irritate you. [Attributed Fred Barling]

Philosophy is a study that lets us be unhappy more intelligently.

There are three schools of magic. One: State a tautology, then ring the changes on its corollaries; that's philosophy. Two: Record many facts. Try to find a pattern. Then make a wrong guess at the next fact; that's science. Three: Be aware what you live in.

Philosophy bakes no bread.

The quoit attracts them more than philosophy.

Philosophy is nothing but common sense in a dress suit.

Whoever laughs at a proposition, before its champion has had a chance to defend it, assumes the burden of proof against it.

A conclusion is what you reach when you get tired of thinking.

When science finally locates the center of the universe, some people will be surprised to learn they're not it.

The only difference between graffiti and philosophy is the word 'fuck.'

Isaac Asimov

⊢ 1920—1992 *American science-fiction writer*

Jokes of the proper kind, properly told, can do more to enlighten questions of politics, philosophy, and literature than any number of dull arguments.

University President: 'Why is it that you physicists always require so much expensive equipment? Now the Department of Mathematics requires nothing but money for paper, pencils, and erasers ... and the Department of Philosophy is better still. It doesn't even ask for erasers.'

A subtle thought that is in error may yet give rise to fruitful inquiry that can establish truths of great value.

The most exciting phrase to hear in science, the one that heralds new discoveries, is not 'Eureka!' (I've found it!), but 'That's funny ...'.

If knowledge can create problems, it is not through ignorance that we can solve them.

Individual science-fiction stories may seem as trivial as ever to the blinder critics and philosophers of today—but the core of science-fiction, its essence has become crucial to our salvation if we are to be saved at all. —[4]

Alfred J. Ayer

⊢ 1910—1989 *English philosopher*

... what is important to us to realize is that even the utterances of the metaphysician who is attempting to expound a vision are literally senseless; so that henceforth we may pursue philosophical researches with as little regard for them as for the more inglorious kind of metaphysics which comes from a failure to understand the workings of our language. —[5]: 29

William E. Aytoun

⊢ 1813—1865 *American poet*

[On metaphysics] An elaborate, dialogical invention for mystifying what was clear, and confounding what was intelligible. —[6]

Francis Bacon

⊢ 1561—1626 *English philosopher*

[On philosophers] The servants of posterity. —[224]

The true philosophical temperament may, we think, be described in four words: much hope, little faith; a disposition to believe that anything, however extraordinary, may be done; an indisposition to believe that anything extraordinary has been done. —[224]

History make men wise; poets witty; the mathematics subtle; natural philosophy deep; moral grave; logic and rhetoric able to contend. —[8]: *Of Studies*

It is true, that a little philosophy inclineth man's mind to atheism, but depth in philosophy bringeth men's minds about to religion. —[224]

Philosophy, when superficially studied, excites doubt; when thoroughly explored, it dispels it. —[8]

Truth comes out of error more readily than out of confusion. —[7]: *Novum Organum*

Those who have handled sciences have been either men of experiment or men of dogmas. The men of experiment are like the ant: they only collect and use; the reasoners resemble spiders, who make cobwebs out of their own substance. But the bee takes the middle course; it gathers its material from the flowers of the garden and of the field, but transforms and digests it by a power of its own. Not unlike this is the true business of philosophy ... —[224]

Roger Bacon

⊢ 1220—1292 *English philosopher*

Ignorant persons love universals. —[9]: II, 86

Farewell, [Aristotelian] *genera* and *species*! How could they bring about anything? They are monsters. —[98]: 299

Walter Bagehot

⊢ 1826—1877 *English social scientist*

Great and terrible systems of divinity and philosophy lie round about us, which, if true, might drive a wise man mad. —[83]: 17

Mikhail A. Bakunin

⊢ 1814—1876   *Russian revolutionary*

[On metaphysics] The science of any half-lie.

Renford Bambrough

⊢ 1926—1999   *English philosopher*

Philosophers are often too limited in their consideration of a concept because they think primarily or only of the contexts and occasions of the use of the most general word that we have for expressing it. To understand causation is not just to be able to analyse propositions of the form '*A* causes *B*' but to know what we are doing when we speak of cooking, burning, shooting, insulting, dissapointing, cutting a cake or a dash or an acquaintance. —[11]

George Bataille

⊢ 1897—1962   *French philosopher*

[F]or academic men to be happy, the universe would have to take shape. All of philosophy has no other goal: it is a matter of giving a frock coat to what is, a mathematical frock coat. On the other hand, affirming that the universe resembles nothing and is only formless amounts to saying that the universe is something like a spider or spit. —[12]

Reprinted by the kind permission of University of Minnesota Press.

Henry Ward Beecher

⊢ 1813—1887   *American clergyman*

The philosophy of one century is the common sense of the next.

Ludwig van Beethoven

⊢ 1770—1827   *German-Austrian composer*

Music is a higher revelation than philosophy.

Jeremy Bentham

⊢ 1748—1832   *English philosopher*

O Logic: Born gatekeeper to the Temple of Science, victim of capricious destiny: doomed hitherto to be the drudge of pedants: come to the aid of thy master, Legislation. —[13]

Nicolas Berdyaev

⊢ 1874—1948 *Russian philosopher*

All the tensions and contradictions in life are, and ought to be, reflected in one's philosophy, and one should not attempt to compose them for the sake of the neat philosophical construction. Philosophy cannot ever be divorced from the totality of man's spiritual experience, from his struggles, his insights, his ecstasies, his religious faith and mystical vision. —[14]

John Berger

⊢ 1926— *English novelist, playwright, and art critic*

The human imagination ... has great difficulty in living strictly within the confines of a materialist practice or philosophy. It dreams, like a dog in its basket, of hares in the open. —[15]

Henri Bergson

⊢ 1859—1941 *French philosopher*

The only cure for vanity is laughter, and the only fault that's laughable is vanity.

Think like a man of action, act like a man of thought.

George Berkeley

⊢ 1685—1753 *Irish philosopher*

Upon the whole, I am inclined to think that the far greater part, if not all, of those difficulties which have hitherto amused philosophers, and blocked up the way to knowledge, are entirely owing to ourselves. We have first raised a dust, and then complain we cannot see. —[16]: §3

Few men think, yet all have opinions. —[16]: *Three Dialogues* (2nd dialogue)

Isaiah Berlin

⊢ 1909—1997 *English social historian, philosopher and essayist*

[On philosophers] Adults who persist in asking childish questions.

'What is an okapi?' is answered easily enough by an act of empirical observation. Similarly 'What is the cube root of 729'? is settled by a piece of calculation in accordance with accepted rule. But if I ask 'What is the time?', 'What is a number?', 'What is the purpose of human life on earth?' ..., how do I set about looking for the answer? ...
    The only common characteristic which all these questions appear to have is that they cannot be answered either by observation or calculation, either by inductive methods or deductive; and as a crucial corollary of this, that those who ask them are faced with a perplexity from the very beginning—they do

not know where to look for the answers; there are no dictionaries, encyclopedias, compendia of knowledge, no experts, no orthodoxies, which can be referred to with the confidence as possessing unquestionable authority or knowledge of these matters. Moreover some of these questions are distinguished by being general and dealing with matters in principle; and others, while not themselves general, very readily raise or lead to questions of principle.

Such questions tend to be called philosophical. —[17]: 2

On behalf of the Isaiah Berlin Literary Trust. © Isaiah Berlin 1962.

Ambrose Bierce

⊢ 1842—1914   *American journalist*

PHILOSOPHY, n. A route of many roads leading from nowhere to nothing. —[18]

All are lunatics, but he who can analyze his delusion is called a philosopher. —[18]

INNATE, adj. Natural, inherent – as innate ideas ... that we are born with ... . The doctrine of innate ideas is one of the most admirable faiths of philosophy, being itself an innate idea and therefore inaccessible to disproof. —[18]

TRUTH, n. An ingenious compound of desirability and appearance. Discovery of truth is the sole purpose of philosophy, which is the most ancient occupation of the human mind and has a fair prospect of existing ... to the end of time. —[18]

GNOSTICS, n. A sect of philosophers who tried to engineer a fusion between the early Christians and the Platonists. The former would not go into the caucus and the combination failed, greatly to the chagrin of the fusion managers. —[18]

CARTESIAN, adj. Relating to Descartes, a famous philosopher, author of the celebrated dictum, 'Cogito ergo sum' – whereby he was pleased to suppose he demonstrated the reality of human existence. The dictum might be improved, however, thus: 'Cogito cogito ergo cogito sum' – "I think that I think, therefore I think that I am;" as close an approach to certainty as any philosopher has yet made. —[18]

ABSURDITY, n. A statement or belief manifestly inconsistent with one's own opinion. —[18]

ACADEME, n. An ancient school where morality and philosophy were taught. ACADEMY, n. A modern school where football is taught. —[18]

LOGIC, n. The art of thinking and reasoning in strict accordance with the limitations and incapacities of the human misunderstanding. —[18]

Antoinette Brown Blackwell

⊢ 1825—1921 *American minister and reformer*

A woman finds the natural lay of the land almost unconsciously; and not feeling it incumbent on her to be guide and philosopher to any successor, she takes little pains to mark the route by which she is making her ascent. —[19]

Marguerite Blessington

⊢ 1789—1849   *Irish writer*

Modern historians are all would-be philosophers; who, instead of relating facts as they occurred, give us their version, or rather perversions of them, always colored by their political prejudices, or distorted to establish some theory ... —[20]

Ned Block

⊢ 1942—   *American philosopher*

You ask: What is it that philosophers have called qualitative states? I answer, only half in jest: As Louis Armstrong is said to have said when asked what jazz is, 'If you got to ask, you ain't never gonna get to know'. —[21]

Niels Bohr

⊢ 1842—1914   *Danish physicist*

An expert is someone who starts out knowing something about some things, goes on to know more and more about less and less, and ends up knowing everything about nothing. Whereas a philosopher is someone who starts out knowing something about some things, goes on to know less and less about more and more, and ends up knowing nothing about everything. — [10]: 421

I have made a great discovery, a very great discovery: all that philosophers have ever written is pure drivel. —[10]: 421

Edward de Bono

⊢ 1933— *Maltese educator*

It has always surprised me how little attention philosophers have paid to humor, since it is a more significant process of mind than reason. Reason can only sort out perceptions, but the humor process is involved in changing them. —[22]

Daniel J. Boorstin

⊢ 1934—1986 *American historian and public servant*

The greatest obstacle to discovery is not ignorance—it is the illusion of knowledge.

Marx Born

⊢ 1882—1970 *German physicist*

I am now convinced that theoretical physics is actually philosophy. —[24]

There are two objectionable types of believers: those who believe the incredible and those who believe that 'belief' must be discarded and replaced by 'the scientific method.' —[25]: Appendix 1

James Boswell

⊢ 1882—1970 *American writer*

After we came out of the church, we stood talking for some time together of Bishop Berkeley's ingenious sophistry to prove the non-existence of matter, and that everything in the universe is merely ideal. I observed, that though we are satisfied his doctrine is not true, it is impossible to refute it. I never shall forget the alacrity with which Johnson answered, striking his foot with mighty force against a large stone, till he rebounded from it, 'I refute it thus.' —[26]

Francis Herbert Bradley

⊢ 1846—1924 *English philosopher*

Metaphysics is the finding of bad reasons for what we believe upon instinct. —[28]: Preface

Mel Brooks

⊢ 1926— *American actor and director*

Look, I really don't want to wax philosophic, but I will say that if you're alive, you got to flap your arms and legs, you got to jump around a lot, you got to make a lot of noise ... , or at least your thoughts should be noisy and colorful and lively.

Joyce Brothers

⊢ 1949— *American psychologist, author and columnist*

A philosopher is a person who doesn't care which side his bread is buttered on; he knows he eats both sides anyway. —[29]

Charlie Brown

⊢ *American cartoon figure*

I've developed a new philosophy ... I only dread one day at a time.

Thomas Browne

⊢ 1605—1682   *English physician and author*

To believe only possibilities, is not faith, but mere Philosophy.

The severe schools shall never laugh me out of the philosophy of Hermes, that this visible world is but a picture of the invisible, wherein as in a portrait, things are not truly, but in equivocal shapes, and as they counterfeit some real substance in that invisible fabric.

Giordano Bruno

⊢ 1548—1600   *Italian philosopher*

Consequently, that beautiful [Aristotelian] order and ladder of nature is but a charming dream, an old wives' tale. —[30]: 239

Make then your forecasts, my lord Astrologers, with your slavish physicians, by means of those astrolabes with which you seek to discern the fantastic nine moving spheres; in these you finally imprison your own minds, so that you appear to me but as parrots in a cage, while I watch you dancing up and down, turning and hopping within those circles. —[30]: 245

Edward Bulwer-Lytton

⊢ 1803—1873   *English novelist and poet*

'Know thyself,' said the old philosopher, 'improve thyself,' said the new. Our great object in time is not to waste our passions and gifts on the things external that we must leave behind, but that we cultivate within us all that we can carry into the eternal progress beyond.

He who esteems trifles for themselves is a trifler; he who esteems them for the conclusions to be drawn from them, or the advantage to which they can be put, is a philosopher.

Vannevar Bush

⊢ 1890—1974   *American scientist*

A belief may be larger than a fact.

Samuel Butler

⊢ 1612—1680   *English writer*

Philosophy is like stirring mud or not letting a sleeping dog lie. —[31]

Beside, he was a shrewd philosopher,
And had read ev'ry text and gloss over

Whate'er the crabbed'st author hath,
He understood b' implicit faith.
—[31]: (pt. I, canto I, l. 127)

3   C

Thomas Campbell

⊢   1777—1844   *Scottish poet and journalist*

Triumphal arch, that fill'st the sky
When storms prepare to part,
I ask not proud Philosophy
To teach me what thou art. —[32]

Albert Camus

⊢   1913—1960   *French philosopher*

There is but one truly serious philosophical problem, and that is suicide. Judging whether life is or is not worth living amounts to answering the fundamental question of philosophy. —[33]

A novel is never anything but a philosophy put into images.

Elias Canetti

⊢ 1905—1994   *Bulgarian-German novelist, essayist, sociologist, and playwright*

The profoundest thoughts of the philosophers have something tricklike about them. A lot disappears in order for something to suddenly appear in the palm of the hand. —[34]

Thomas Carlyle

⊢ 1795—1881   *Scottish historian, and sociological writer*

Metaphysics is the attempt of the mind to rise above the mind. —[35]

What is philosophy but a continual battle against custom?

Before philosophy can teach by Experience, the Philosophy has to be in readiness, the Experience must be gathered and intelligibly recorded. —[36]

Rudolf Carnap

⊢ 1891—1970   *German-American philosopher*

But we give no answer to philosophical questions, and instead *reject all philosophical questions*, whether of Metaphysics, Ethics or Epistemology. For our is with *Logical Analysis*. If that is still to be called Philosophy let it be so; but it involves excluding from consideration all the traditional problems of Philosophy. —[37]: 22

Logic is the last scientific ingredient of Philosophy; its extraction leaves behind only a confusion of non-scientific, pseudo problems. —[37]: 22

Rachel Carson

⊢ 1907—1964 *American author*

Under the philosophy that now seems to guide our destinies, nothing must get in the way of the man with the spray gun. —[38]

Sebastian-Roch-Nicholas Chamfort

⊢ 1741—1794 *French author*

Philosophy, like medicine, has plenty of drugs, few good remedies, and hardly any specific cure. —[39]: vol. 1, no. 17

Alexander Chase

⊢ 1926— *American journalist*

Psychiatry's chief contribution to philosophy is the discovery that the toilet is the seat of the soul. —[40]

John Cheever

⊢ 1912—1982 *American novelist and short-story writer*

People look for morals in fiction because there has always been a confusion between fiction and philosophy.

G.K. Chesterton

⊢ 1874—1936 *English writer*

When all philosophies shall fail,
This word alone shall fit;
That a sage feels too small for life,
And a fool too large for it. —[42]

Reprinted by permission of A.P. Watt on behalf of The Royal Literary Fund.

You can only find truth with logic if you have already found it without it.

The modern habit of saying, 'Every man has a different philosophy; this is my philosophy and it suits me'—the habit of saying this is mere weak mindedness. A cosmic philosophy is not constructed to fit a man; a cosmic philosophy is constructed to fit a cosmos. A man can no more possess a private religion than he can possess a private sun and moon. —[41]

Marcus Tullius Cicero

⊢ 106—43 BC   *Roman orator and statesman*

Nothing so absurd can be said that some philosopher had not said it. —[43]

Reprinted by permission of the publishers and the Trustees of the Loeb Classical Library from Cicero: Volume XX, Loeb Classical Library Vol. 154, translated by W.A. Falconer, Cambridge, Mass.: Harvard University Press, 1923. The Loeb Classical Library ® is a registered trademark of the President and Fellows of Harvard College.

We are motivated by a keen desire for praise, and the better a man is the more he is inspired by glory. The very philosophers themselves, even in those books which they write in contempt of glory, inscribe their names. —[43]

Reprinted by permission of the publishers and the Trustees of the Loeb Classical Library from Cicero: Volume XX, Loeb Classical Library Vol. 154, translated by W.A. Falconer, Cambridge, Mass.: Harvard University Press, 1923. The Loeb Classical Library ® is a registered trademark of the President and Fellows of Harvard College.

For what is more unbecoming to a wise man than to judge rashly? Or what rashness is so unworthy of the gravity and stability of a philosopher, as either to maintain false opinions, or without the least hesitation to support and defend what he has not thoroughly examined, and does not clearly comprehend. —[44]

Socrates was the first to call philosophy down from the heavens and to place it in cities, and even to introduce it into homes and compel it to enquire about life and standards and good and ill.
—[45]

Arthur C. Clarke

⊢ 1917— *American science-fiction writer*

When a distinguished but elderly scientist states that something is possible, he is almost certainly right. When he states that something is impossible, he is very probably wrong. —[46]

Samuel T. Coleridge

⊢ 1772—1834 *English poet, critic, and philosopher*

Common sense in an uncommon degree is what the world calls wisdom.

The wise only possess ideas; the greater part of mankind are possessed by them.

John Churton Collins

⊢ 1848—1908 *English writer*

Truth is the object of philosophy, but not always of philosophers.

Anne Finch Conway

⊢ 1631—1679 *English philosopher*

From what hath been lately said, and from the diverse Reactions alledged, That Spirit and Body are originally in their first Substance but one and the same thing, it evidently appears that the Philosophers (so called) which have taught otherwise, whether Ancient or Modern, have generally erred and laid an ill Foundation in the very beginning, whence the whole House and superstructure is so feeble, and indeed so unprofitable, that the whole Edifice and Building must in time decay, from which absurd Foundation have arose very many gross and dangerous Errours, not only in Philosophy but also in Divinity ... —[48]: 221

Mason Cooley

⊢ 1927— *American aphorist*

Philosophy likes to keen common sense on the run. —[49]

Libby Copeland

⊢ *American journalist*

Here's what's wild: Philosophy is hot nowadays, hot as, say, Ricky Martin in leather. —[50]

© 2001, The Washington Post. Reprinted with permission.

Victor Cousin

⊢ 1792—1867   *French philosopher*

True philosophy invents nothing; it merely establishes and describes what is.

Stephen Crane

⊢ 1871—1900   *American writer and poet*

Philosophy should always know that indifference is a militant thing. —[51]

David Cronenberg

⊢ 1943—   *American director*

When you're in the muck you can only see muck. If you somehow manage to float above it, you still see the muck but you see it from a different perspective. And you see other things too. That's the consolation of philosophy. —[52]: Ch. 3

4 D

Jean D'Alembert

⊢ 1717—1783 *French physicist and philosopher*

[On a philosopher] A fool who torments himself while he is alive, to be talked about after he is dead.

Daniel C. Dennett

⊢ 1942— *American philosopher*

When philosophical fantasies become too outlandish – involving time machines, say, or duplicate universes or infinitely powerful deceiving demons – we may wisely decline to conclude anything from them. Our conviction that we understand the issues involved may be unreliable, an illusion produced by the vividness of the fantasy. —[54]

To him it was obvious that Professor Dennett was just inventing another of his wild science-fiction fantasies, yet another intuition pump to bamboozle the gullible. —[53]: 3-4

No one wants to learn that one's crusading career is just half of a tempest in a teapot, and so philosophers are typically not eager to accept ... bland and ecumenical resolutions of their controversies, but it can be reassuring, and even enlightening – if not especially exciting – to remind ourselves of just how much fundamental agreement there is. —[53]: 340

We are all standing around each other's data, looking in roughly the same directions for roughly the same things. Priority squabbles may make sense in some disciplines, but in philosophy they tend to take on the air of disputes among the sailors about who gets credit for first noticing that the breeze has come up. —[53]: 350

There is no such thing as philosophy-free science; there is only science whose philosophical baggage is taken on board without examination.

A scholar is just a library's way of making another library.

Out of the Armchair and Into the Field. —[55]

René Descartes

⊢ 1596—1650 *French philosopher and scientist*

Having learned from the time I was at school that there is nothing one can imagine so strange or so unbelievable that it has not been said by one or other of the philosophers; and since then, while travelling, having recognized that those who hold opinions quite opposed to ours are not on that account barbarians or savages, but that many exercise as much reason as we do, or more; and having considered how a given man, with his given mind, being brought up from childhood among the French or Germans becomes different from what he would be if he had always lived among the Chinese or among the cannibals ... I was convinced that our beliefs are based much more on custom and example than on any certain knowledge. —[56]

Reprinted by the kind permission of the publisher from Descartes, R. DISCOURSE ON THE METHOD AND MEDITATIONS ON FIRST PHILOSOPHY, edited by David Weissman. Copyright © 1996 by Yale University Press.

Good sense is the best distributed thing in the world: for everyone thinks himself so well endowed with it that even those who are the hardest to please in everything else do not usually desire more of it than they possess. —[56]

Reprinted by the kind permission of the publisher from Descartes, R. DISCOURSE ON THE METHOD AND MEDITATIONS ON FIRST PHILOSOPHY, edited by David Weissman. Copyright © 1996 by Yale University Press.

It is not enough to have a good mind. The main thing is to use it well. —[56]

Reprinted by the kind permission of the publisher from Descartes, R. DISCOURSE ON THE METHOD AND MEDITATIONS ON FIRST PHILOSOPHY, edited by David Weissman. Copyright © 1996 by Yale University Press.

Philosophy has been studied for many centuries by the most outstanding minds without having produced anything which is not in dispute. —[56]

Reprinted by the kind permission of the publisher from Descartes, R. DISCOURSE ON THE METHOD AND MEDITATIONS ON FIRST PHILOSOPHY, edited by David Weissman. Copyright © 1996 by Yale University Press.

John Dewey

⊢ 1859—1952   *American philosopher*

Man is not logical and his intellectual history is a record of mental reserves and compromises. He hangs on to what he can in his old beliefs even when he is compelled to surrender their logical basis. —[58]

Denis Diderot

⊢ 1713—1784   *French philosopher*

For the philosopher, posterity is what the after-world is for the religious man. —[59]

The philosopher has never killed any priests, whereas the priest has killed a great many philosophers. —[60]

The first step towards philosophy is incredulity.

Diogenes [the Cynic]

⊢ ca. 400—ca. 325 BC   *Greek philosopher*

For the answer was good that Diogenes made to one that asked him in mockery How it came to pass that philosophers were the followers of rich men, and not rich men of philosophers He answered soberly, and yet sharply, Because the one sort knew what they had need of, and the other did not. —[61]

Reprinted by permission of the publishers and the Trustees of the Loeb Classical Library from Diogenes Laertius: Volume I, Loeb Classical Library Vol. 84, translated by R.D. Hicks, Cambridge, Mass.: Harvard University Press, 1925. The Loeb Classical Library ® is a registered trademark of the President and Fellows of Harvard College.

Of what use is a philosopher who doesn't hurt anybody's feelings? —[61]

Reprinted by permission of the publishers and the Trustees of the Loeb Classical Library from Diogenes Laertius: Volume I, Loeb Classical Library Vol. 84, translated by R.D. Hicks, Cambridge, Mass.: Harvard University Press, 1925. The Loeb Classical Library ® is a registered trademark of the President and Fellows of Harvard College.

Michele Le Doeuff

⊢ 1948— *French philosopher*

The simple fact that philosophical discourse is a discipline is sufficient to show that something is repressed within it. But what is repressed? ... Philosophy creates itself in what is repressed. —[62]

The irony is that the creative areas in philosophy today do not lie in the region of academic work. —[62]

Lord Dunsany

⊢ 1878—1957 *English playwright and author*

Logic, like whisky, loses its beneficial effect when taken in too large quantities. —[63]

Ariel Durant

⊢ 1898—1981 *American historian and philosopher*

It is good a philosopher should remind himself, now and then, that he is a particle pontificating on infinity. —[64]

Will Durant

⊢ 1885—1981 *American historian and philosopher*

[The early Greek philosophers] asked questions about anything; they stood unafraid in the presence of religious or political taboos; and boldly subpoenaed every creed and institution to appear before the judgment-seat of reason. —[65]

Oliver Edwards

⊢ 1711—1791   *English lawyer*

I have tried too in my time to be a philosopher; but, I don't know how, cheerfulness was always breaking in. —[26]

Paul Edwards

⊢ 1923—   *American philosopher*

Heidegger's ... *Introduction to Metaphysics* was written in 1935 and compared to what was to follow it is a model of lucidity and concision ... No matter what the starting point of a discussion is in the later works, whether it is a passage from Parmenides, a poem of Hölderlin or a quotation from Nietzsche, the end is always the same: Being '*west*', the Presence presences, Being conceals itself but reveals itself in its very concealment or the other way around, the Appropriation appropriates ... and of course the basic fact that beings are not Being. In between you get bogus Greek and German etymologies which would prove nothing even if they were not bogus and all kinds of gimmicks including the constant breaking up of German words (what Sheehan had aptly called 'hyphenitis') and the coinage of new words which remain totally unexplained. As a result we are given huge masses of hideous gibberish which must be unique in the history of philosophy. —[66]

... Heidegger will continue to fascinate those hungry for mysticism of the anaemic and purely verbal variety, the 'glossogonous metaphysics' of which his philosophy is such an outstanding example. ... More sober and rational persons will continue to regard the whole Heidegger phenomenon as a grotesque aberration of the human mind. —[66]

Albert Einstein

⊢ 1879—1955   *German-Swiss-American theoretical physicist*

When I study philosophical works I feel I am swallowing something which I don't have in my mouth. —[160]

God does not care about mathematical difficulties: He integrates empirically. —[160]

Our age is characterized by perfecting the means, while confusing the goals. —[67]

The physicist cannot simply surrender to the philosopher the critical contemplation of the theoretical foundations; for he himself knows best and feels most surely where the shoe pinches ... He must try to make clear in his own mind just how far the concepts which he uses are justified ... The whole of science is nothing more than a refinement of everyday thinking. —[67]

If most of us are ashamed of shabby clothes and shoddy furniture, let us be more ashamed of shabby ideas and shoddy philosophies. —[67]

As for the search for truth, I know from my own painful searching, with its many blind alleys, how hard it is to take a reliable step, be it ever so small, towards the understanding of that which is truly significant. —[67]

George Eliot

⊢ 1819—1880   *English author*

But human experience is usually paradoxical, that means incongruous with the phrases of current talk or even current philosophy. —[70]: Bk. 8, ch. 69

Plain women he regarded as he did the other severe facts of life, to be faced with philosophy and investigated by science. —[69]

Thomas Stearns Eliot

⊢ 1888—1965   *English poet and writer*

A philosophy can and must be worked out with the greatest rigour and discipline in the details, but can ultimately be founded on nothing but faith: and this is the reason, I suspect, why the novelties in philosophy are only in elaboration, and never in fundamentals. —[70]: Ch. 7

Hugh Elliot

⊢ 1752—1830 *Scottish diplomat*

Science therefore, alone can furnish the data of philosophy. If there is any knowledge attainable that can truly be called philosophic, it is such knowledge only as is yielded by a study of the various sciences. Consequently, the first thing to be done in any search after philosophic principles is to travel over the special sciences with a view to extracting from them such information as is relevant to our purpose. —[72]: 300

Ralph Waldo Emerson

⊢ 1803—1882 *American poet and essayist*

A foolish consistency is the hobgoblin of little minds, adored by little statesmen and philosophers and divines.

It is only known to Plato that we can do without Plato. —[73]

Which was the best age of philosophy? That in which there were yet no philosophers.

Art is a jealous mistress, and, if a man have a genius for painting, poetry, music, architecture or philosophy, he makes a bad husband and an ill provider. —[76]

Great geniuses have the shortest biographies. —[74]

Skepticism is slow suicide.

Epictetus

⊢ 55—135 *Roman philosopher*

The essence of philosophy is that a man should so live that his happiness shall depend as little as possible on external things. —[78]

All philosophy lies in two words: Sustain and Abstain. —[78]

The beginning of philosophy is to know the condition of one's own mind. If a man recognizes that this is in a weakly state, he will not then want to apply it to questions of the greatest moment. As it is, men who are not fit to swallow even a morsel, buy whole treatises and try to devour them. Accordingly they either vomit them up again, or suffer from indigestion, whence come gripings, fluxions, and fevers. Whereas they should have stopped to consider their capacity. —[78]

If a man would pursue Philosophy, his first task is to throw away conceit. For it is impossible for a man to begin to learn what he has a conceit that he already knows. —[78]

And I think all will allow that one who proposes to hear philosophers speak needs a considerable training in hearing. Is that not so? Then tell me on what subject you are able to hear me. —[78]

What concerns me is not the way things are, but rather the way people think things are. —[78]

We must not believe the many, who say that only free people ought to be educated, but we should rather believe the philosophers who say that only the educated are free. —[78]

The Beginning of Philosophy ... is a Consciousness of your own Weakness and inability in necessary things. —[78]

Nominis Expers

The wiser man, recognizing Buddha's ontological error, decides not to remain a consistent philosophical ostrich, suspends his forced and temporary absurd denial of the empirical evidence of sense perception, and using his faculty of reason, re-calibrates his ontology to allow for the reality of traffic when crossing the street, thereby escaping suffering.

Ludwig Feurbach

⊢ 1804—1872 *German philosopher*

How the philosophers have tortured themselves with the question as to where and with what philosophy begins ... Oh, you fools, who open your mouth in sheer wonder over the enigmas of the beginning and yet fail to see that the open mouth is the entrance to the heart of nature: who fail to see that your teeth have long ago cracked the nut upon which you are still breaking your heads. We begin to think with that with which we begin to exist. The principium essendi is also the principium cognoscendi. But the beginning of existence is nourishment; therefore, food is the beginning of wisdom. The first condition of putting any thing into your head and heart, is to put something into your stomach. —[122]

Paul Feyerabend

⊢ 1924—1994 *Austrian philosopher*

There is no idea, however ancient and absurd, that is not capable of improving our knowledge. The whole history of thought is absorbed into science and is used for improving every single theory. —[79]

Science is much closer to myth than a scientific philosophy is prepared to admit. It is one of the many forms of thought that has been developed by man, and not necessarily the best. It is conspicuous, noisy, and impudent, but it is inherently superior only for those who have already decided in favor of a certain ideology, or who have accepted it without ever having examined its advantages and its limits. —[79]

Richard P. Feynman

⊢ 1918—1988 *American theoretical physicist*

Philosophers, incidentally, say a great deal about what is absolutely necessary for science, and it is always, so far as one can see, rather naive and probably wrong. —[81]

My son is taking a course in philosophy, and last night we were looking at something by Spinoza—and there was the most childish reasoning! There were all these Attributes, and Substances, all this meaningless chewing around, and we started to laugh. Now how could we do that? Here's this great Dutch philosopher, and we're laughing at him. It's because there is no excuse for it! In the same period there was Newton, there was Harvey studying the circulation of the blood, there were people with methods of analysis by which progress was made! You can take every one of Spinoza's propositions and take the contrary propositions, and look at the world—and you can't tell which is right. Sure, people were awed because he had the courage to take on these great questions, but it doesn't do any good to have the courage if you can't get anywhere with the question. —[82]

It isn't philosophy that gets me, it's the pomposity. If they'd just laugh at themselves. If they'd just say, 'I think it's like this, but von Leipzig thought it was like that, and he had a good shot at it, too'. If they'd explain that this is their best guess ... But so few of them do; instead, they seize on the possibility that there may not be an ultimate fundamental particle, and say that you should stop work and ponder with great profundity: 'You haven't thought deeply enough, first let me define the world for you'. Well, I'm going to investigate it without defining it! —[82]

A philosopher once said 'It is necessary for the very existence of science that the same conditions always produce the same results'. Well, they do not. You set up the circumstances, with the same conditions every time, and you cannot predict behind which hole you will see the electron. —[81]

I believe that a scientist looking at non-scientific problems is just as dumb as the next guy.

Melvin Fitting

⊢ 1942— *American logician and philosopher*

Of course I believe that solipsism is the correct philosophy, but that's only one man's opinion.
—[Said to Raymond M. Smullyan]

Anthony Flew

⊢ 1923— *English philosopher*

In the ordinary, everyday understandings of the words involved, to say that someone survived death is to contradict yourself;

while to assert that all of us live forever is to assert a manifest falsehood, the flat contrary of a universally known truth: namely, the truth that all human beings are mortal. For when, after some disaster, the 'dead' and the 'survivors' have both been listed, what logical space remains for a third category? —[84]

Jerry Fodor

⊢ 1935— *American philosopher*

It is a curiosity of the philosophical temperament, this passion for radical solutions. Do you feel a little twinge in your epistemology? Absolute skepticism is the thing to try. Has the logic of confirmation got you down? Probably physics is fiction. Worried about individuating objects? Don't let anything in but sets. Nobody has yet suggested that the way out of the Liar paradox is to give up talking, but I expect it's only a matter of time. Apparently the rule is this: if aspirin doesn't work, try cutting of your head. —[85]: 420

La Bovier de Fontenelle

⊢ 1657—1757 *French writer*

[On a philosopher] A person who will not believe what he sees because he is too busy speculating about what he does not see.

Benjamin Franklin

⊢ 1706—1790   *American statesman, inventor, philanthropist and publisher*

God grant that not only the love of liberty but a thorough knowledge of the rights of man may pervade all the nations of the earth, so that a philosopher may set his foot anywhere on its surface and say: 'This is my country.' —[86]

You philosophers are sages in your maxims, and fools in your conduct. —[86]

Gottlob Frege

⊢ 1848—1925   *German logician, mathematician and philosopher*

A scientist can hardly meet with anything more undesirable than to have the foundations give way just as the work is finished. I was put in this position by a letter from Mr. Bertrand Russell when the work was nearly through the press. —[88]

James A. Froude

⊢ 1818—1894   *English essayist and historian*

Philosophy goes no further than probabilities, and in every assertion keeps a doubt in reserve.

John Kenneth Galbraith

⊢ 1908— *American economist*

The modern conservative is engaged in one of man's oldest exercises in moral philosophy; that is, the search for a superior moral justification for selfishness. —[90]

Galileo Galilei

⊢ 1564—1642 *Italian astronomer and physicist*

Philosophy is written in this grand book. I mean the universe—which stands continually open to our gaze, but it cannot be understood unless one first learns to comprehend the language and interpret the characters in which it is written. It is written in the language of mathematics, and its characters are triangles, circles, and other geometrical figures, without which it is humanly impossible to understand a single word of it. —[91]

I wish, my dear Kepler, that we could have a good laugh together at the extraordinary stupidity of the mob. What do you think of the foremost philosophers at this University? In spite of my oft-repeated efforts and invitations, they have refused, with the obstinacy of a glutted adder, to look at the planets or the Moon or my glasses. —[91]

To pretend that truth is so deeply hidden from us and that it is hard to distinguish it from falsehood is quite preposterous: the truth remains hidden only while we have nothing but false opinions and doubtful speculations; but hardly has truth made its appearance than its light will dispel dark shadows. —[92]

John W. Gardner

⊢ 1912— *American educator and philanthropist*

The society which scorns excellence in plumbing as a humble activity and tolerates shoddiness in philosophy because it is an exaulted activity will have neither good plumbing nor good philosophy ... neither its pipes nor its theories will hold water. —[93]

José Ortega y Gassett

⊢ 1883—1955 *Spanish philosopher*

Philosophy has always gone astray by giving the name 'I' to the most unlikely things, but never to the thing you call 'I' in daily life. —[95]

Paul Gauguin

⊢   1848—1903   *French painter*

Art requires philosophy, just as philosophy requires art. Otherwise, what would become of beauty? —[94]

Ernest Gellner

⊢   1925—   *English philosopher, anthropologist, and sociologist*

A cleric who loses his faith abandons his calling, a philosopher who loses his redefines his subject. —[97]: 259

William E. Gladstone

⊢   1883—1931   *English prime minister*

Men are apt to mistake the strength of their feeling for the strength of their argument. The heated mind resents the chill touch and relentless scrutiny of logic. —[99]

Kahlil Gibran

⊢ 1883—1931 *Lebanese poet, philosopher, and artist*

Keep me away from the wisdom which does not cry, the philosophy which does not laugh and the greatness which does not bow before children.

Clark Glymour

⊢ *American philosopher*

A second contemporary approach to skepticism and the problems of knowledge, an approach that can best be called primitivism [Heidegger, Sartre, Merleau-Ponty], rejects the concern for rational, true belief that such problems presuppose ... — [100]

Primitivism doesn't have much to offer those interested in the possibilities and limits of knowledge, in how we must be constituted and how the world must be constituted for us to know the world, in the nature of reason, demonstration and meaning, in how the phenomena of mind can arise in a mindless world. Indeed, primitivists do not want to offer any results about these topics, nor, often enough, do they want others to. —[100]

Nelson Goodman

⊢ 1906—1998 *American philosopher*

Any effort in philosophy to make the obscure obvious is likely to be unappealing, for the penalty of failure is confusion while the reward of success is banality. An answer, once found, is dull; and the only remaining interest lies in a further effort to render equally dull what is still obscure enough to be interesting. — [103]: xv

Johan Wolfgang von Goethe

⊢ 1749—1832 *German poet, novelist, playwright, courtier, and natural philosopher*

What wise or stupid thing can man conceive. That was not thought of in ages long ago?
—[101]: Second Part, act II, *Gothic Chamber*

Oliver Goldsmith

⊢ 1728—1774 *Irish dramatist*

This same philosophy is a good horse in the stable, but an arrant jade on a journey. —[102]: Act 1

Rebecca Goldstein

⊢ *American philosopher*

The process of thinking about philosophy always reminds me of fireworks. One question is shot up and bursts into a splendorous many. Answers? Forget answers. The spectacle is all in the questions.—[104]

Reprinted with Permission. from THE MIND-BODY PROBLEM by Rebecca Goldstein © 1983, Random House

Catherine the Great

⊢ 1729—1796 *Russian empress*

You philosophers are lucky men. You write on paper and paper is patient. Unfortunate Empress that I am, I write on the susceptible skins of living beings.

Phillip Guedalla

⊢ 1884—1944 *American historian*

Just as philosophy is the study of other people's misconceptions, so history is the study of other peoples mistakes.

8   H

Ian Hacking

⊢ 1936— *Canadian philosopher*

Philosophers long made a mummy of science. When they finally unwrapped the cadaver and saw the remnants of an historical process of becoming and discovering, they created for themselves a crisis of rationality. That happened around 1960.
It was a crisis because it upset our old tradition of thinking that scientific knowledge is the crowning achievement of human reason. Sceptics have always challenged the complacent panorama of cumulative and accumulating human knowledge, but now they took ammunition from the details of history. —[105]

His is a philosophy founded upon reflections on language, and no such philosophy can teach anything positive about natural science. —[105]

William Hamilton

⊢ 1788—1856   *Scottish philosopher*

Truth, like a torch, the more it's shook the more it shines. —[106]

D.W. Hamlyn

⊢ 1924—   *English philosopher*

The life-blood of philosophy is argument and counter-argument. Plato and Aristotle thought of this occurring in what they called dialectic—discussion. Today, it might be argued that it is just the same way, except that it operates upon a much wider scale, both historically and geographically. Argument and counter-argument in books and journals is the modern version of dialectic. —[107]: 333

Christopher Hampton

⊢ 1946—   *English dramatist*

I became a virtuoso of deceit. It wasn't pleasure I was after, it was knowledge. I consulted the strictest moralists to learn how to appear, philosophers to find out what to think and novelists to see what I could get away with. —[108]

Sydney J. Harris

⊢ 1917— *American journalist and author*

Any philosophy that can be put in a nutshell belongs there.

Stephen W. Hawking

⊢ 1942— *English theoretical physicist and cosmologist*

Up to now, most scientists have been too occupied with the development of new theories that describe *what* the universe is to ask the question *why*. On the other hand, the people whose business it is to ask *why*, the philosophers, have not been able to keep up with the advance of scientific theories. In the eighteenth century, philosophers considered the whole of human knowledge, including science, to be their field and discussed questions such as: Did the universe have a beginning? However, in the nineteenth and twentieth centuries, science became too technical and mathematical for the philosophers, or anyone else except a few specialists. Philosophers reduced the scope of their inquiries so much that Wittgenstein, the most famous philosopher of this century, said, 'The sole remaining task for philosophy is the analysis of language.' What a comedown from the great tradition of philosophy from Aristotle and Kant! —[110]: 174

Extract from A BRIEF HISTORY OF TIME by Stephen Hawking published by Bantam Books. Used by permission of the Random House Group Limited.

William Hazlitt

⊢ 1778—1830 *English essayist*

[On the philosopher] One who can forget himself. —[111]

William Randolph Hearst

⊢ 1863—1951 *American newspaper proprietor*

If you make a product good enough ... the public will make a path to your door, says the philosopher. But if you want the public in sufficient numbers, you would better construct a highway. Advertising is that highway. —[23]

Heathiana

⊢ 1889—1951

Philosophy is the art of bewildering oneself methodically. —[47]

Georg Friedrich Hegel

⊢ 1770—1834 *German philosopher*

The soul takes refuge in the realm of thought, and in opposition to the real world it creates a world of ideas. Philosophy begins with the decline of the real world: When she appears with her abstractions, painting grey on grey, then the freshness of youth and life is already gone, and her reconciliation is not one in reality but in an ideal world. —[112]

Every philosophy is essentially idealism or at least has idealism as its principle, and the question then is only how far this principle is actually carried out ... A philosophy which ascribed genuine, ultimate, absolute being to finite existence as such, would not deserve the name philosophy. —[112]

Martin Heidegger

⊢ 1889—1976 *German philosopher*

You do not get to philosophy by reading many and multifarious philosophical books, nor by torturing yourself with solving the riddles of the universe ... philosophy remains latent in every human existence and need not be first added to it from somewhere else. —[113]

Piet Hein

⊢ 1905—1996 *Danish poet and scientist*

Philosophers
must ultimately find
their true perfection
in knowing all
the follies of mankind
by introspection. —[114]

Werner Heisenberg

⊢ 1901—1976 *German physicist*

The philosophic thesis that all knowledge is ultimately founded in experience has in the end led to a postulate concerning the logical clarification of any statement about nature. Such a postulate may have seemed justified in the period of classical physics, but since quantum theory we have learned that it cannot be fulfilled. —[115]

We often know that [concepts] can be applied to a wide range of inner or outer experience, but we practically never know precisely the limits of their applicability. This is true even of the simplest and most general concepts like 'existence' and 'space and time'. Therefore, it will never be possible by pure reason to arrive at some absolute truth. —[115]

John Herschel

⊢ 1792—1871 *English astronomer*

Accustomed to trace the operation of general causes, and the exemplification of general laws, in circumstances where the uninformed and unenquiring eye perceives neither novelty nor beauty, [the scientist and natural philosopher] walks in the midst of wonders. —[76]: 124

Abraham Joshua Heschel

⊢ 1907—1972 *Polish-American philosopher*

Philosophy, to be relevant, must offer you a wisdom to live by. —[116]: Chap. 1

From Abraham Joshua Heschel, WHO IS MAN? Copyright © 1965 Abraham Joshua Heschel.

Jaakko Hintikka

⊢ 1929— *Finnish philosopher and logician*

Epistemology seems to enjoy unexpectedly sexy reputation in these days. A few years back William Saffire wrote a popular novel called *The Sleeper Spy*. It depicts a distinctly post-cold-war world in which it is no longer easy to tell the good guys—or, rather, the good spies—from the bad ones. To emphasize this sea change, Saffire tells us that his Russian protagonist has not been trained in the military or the police, as he would have been during the old days, but as an epistemologist. —[117]

Thomas Hobbes

⊢ 1588—1679 *English philosopher*

Leisure is the mother of philosophy. —[118]

Wilfrid Hodges

⊢ *English logician and mathematician*

In English-speaking philosophy (and much European philosophy too) you are taught not to take anything on trust, particularly if it seems obvious and undeniable. You are also taught to criticise anything said by earlier philosophers. Mathematics is not like that; one has to accept some facts as given and not up for arguments. [...] (In the days when I taught philosophy, I remember one student who was told he had failed his course badly. He duly produced a reasoned argument to prove that he hadn't.) —[119]

Other authors, less coherently, suggested that Cantor had used the wrong positive integers. He should have allowed integers which have infinite decimal expansions to the left, like the p-adic integers. To these people I usually sent the comment that they were quite right, the set of real numbers does have the same cardinality as the set of natural numbers in their sense of natural numbers; but the phrase 'natural number' already has a meaning, and that meaning is not theirs. —[119]

Oliver Wendell Holmes, Jr.

⊢ 1841—1935 *American jurist*

Any two philosophers can tell each other all they know in two hours.

Philosophers are men hired by the well-to-do to prove that everything is all right. —[121]: 1

Ted Honderich

⊢ 1933— *American philosopher*

One thinks of French philosophy that it aspires to the condition of literature or the condition of art, and that English and American philosophy aspires to the condition of science. French philosophy, one thinks of as picking up an idea and running with it, possibly into a nearby brick wall or over a local cliff, or something like that. —[120]

Elbert Hubbard

⊢ 1856—1915 *American author and publisher*

[On metaphysics] An attempt to define a thing and by so doing escape the bother of understanding. —[123]

[On the philosopher] One who formulates his prejudices and systematizes his ignorance. —[123]

Logic: an instrument used for bolstering a prejudice. —[123]

David Hume

⊢ 1711—1776   *English philosopher*

Opposing one species of superstition to another, set them a-quarreling; while we ourselves, during their fury and contention, happily make our escape into the calm, though obscure, regions of philosophy. —[128]

Be a philosopher; but amidst your philosophy, be still a man. —[126]

Generally speaking, the errors in religion are dangerous; those in philosophy only ridiculous. —[127]

Thus all probable reasoning is nothing but a species of sensation. 'Tis not solely in poetry and music, we must follow our taste and sentiment, but likewise in philosophy.' —[127]

Nothing appears more surprising to those who consider human affairs with a philosophical eye, than the easiness with which the many are governed by the few. —[125]

Does a man of sense run after every silly tale of hobgoblins or fairies, and canvass particularly the evidence? I never knew anyone, that examined and deliberated about who did not believe it before the end of his enquiries. —[124]

If we take in our hand any volume; of divinity or school metaphysics, for instance; let us ask, 'Does it contain any abstract reasoning concerning quantity or number?' No. 'Does it contain any experimental reasoning concerning matter of fact and existence?' No. Commit it then to the flames: for it can contain nothing but sophistry and illusion.

Aldous Huxley

⊢ 1894—1963 *English novelist and critic*

An unexciting truth may be eclipsed by a thrilling lie. —[129]

Bradley ... defined philosophy as the finding of bad reason for what one believes by instinct. As if anyone believed anything by instinct! One believes things because one has been conditioned to believe them. Finding bad reasons for what one believes for other bad reasons—that's philosophy. —[129]

Thomas Huxley

⊢ 1825—1895 *English biologist*

Cinderella [Science] ... lights the fire, sweeps the house, and provides the dinner; and is rewarded by being told that she is a base creature, devoted to low and material interests. But in her garret she has fairy visions out of the ken of the pair of shrews [Theology and Philosophy] who are quarrelling downstairs. She sees the order which pervades the seeming disorder of the world; the great drama of evolution, with its full share of pity and terror, but also with abundant goodness and beauty ... ; and she learns ... that the foundation of morality is to [be] done, once and for all, with lying; to give up pretending to believe that for which there is no evidence. —[57]: 553

Irish Philosophy of Life

In life, there are only two things to worry about, either you are well, or you are sick.

If you are well, there is nothing to worry about, but if you are sick, you have two things to worry about; either you will live, or you will die.

If you live, there is nothing to worry about, if you die, you have two things to worry about; either you will go to heaven or to hell.

If you go to heaven, there is nothing to worry about, but if you go to hell, you'll be so busy shaking hands with your friends, you won't have time to worry!

10 J

Karl Gustav Jacobi

⊢ 1908—1997 *German mathematician*

It is true that Fourier had the opinion that the principal aim of mathematics was public utility and explanation of natural phenomena; but a philosopher like him should have known that the sole end of science is the honor of the human mind, and that under this title a question about numbers is worth as much as a question about the system of the world. —[131]

William James

⊢ 1842—1910 *American philosopher*

There is only one thing a philosopher can be relied upon to do, and that is to contradict other philosophers. —[134]

Reprinted by permission of the publisher from THE WORKS OF WILLIAM JAMES: ESSAYS IN RADICAL EMPIRICISM, Frederick Burkhardt, General Editor and Fredson Bowers, Textual Editor, Cambridge, Mass.: Harvard University Press, Copyright © 1975 by the President and Fellows of Harvard College.

Philosophy, beginning in wonder ... is able to fancy everything different from what it is. It sees the familiar as if it were strange, and the strange as if it were familiar. It can take things up and lay them down again. Its mind is full of air that plays round every subject. It rouses us from our native dogmatic slumber and breaks up our caked prejudices ... A man with no philosophy in him is the most inauspicious and unprofitable of all possible social mates. —[133]: 'Some Problems of Philosophy'

Philosophy is at once the most sublime and the most trivial of human pursuits. —[133]: Lecture 1

What every genuine philosopher ... craves most is praise—although the philosophers generally call it 'recognition'!
—[136]: Letter to Henri Bergson

To be a real philosopher all that is necessary is to hate some one elses type of thinking.
—[136]: Letter dated 29 January, 1909

Whatever universe a professor believes in must at any rate be a universe that lends itself to lengthy discourse. A universe definable in two sentences is something for which the professorial intellect has no use. No faith in anything of that cheap kind!
—[133]: Lecture 1

... science would be far less advanced than she is if the passionate desires of individuals to get their own faiths confirmed had been kept out of the game. —[132]

Since we are in the main not sceptics, we might go on and frankly confess to each other the motives for our several faiths. I frankly confess mine—I cannot but think that at bottom they are of an aesthetic and not of a logical sort. —[135]

Reprinted by permission of the publisher from THE WORKS OF WILLIAM JAMES: ESSAYS IN RELIGION AND MORALITY, Frederick Burkhardt, General Editor and Fredson Bowers, Textual Editor, Cambridge, Mass.: Harvard University Press, Copyright © 1982 by the President and Fellows of Harvard College.

Metaphysics means nothing but an unusually obstinate attempt to think clearly. —[132]

Objective evidence and certitude are doubtless very fine ideals to play with, but where on this moonlit and dream-visited planet are they found? —[132]

Samuel Johnson

⊢ 1709—1784 *English essayist, lexicographer, poet, and editor*

I have Socrates on my side. It was his labour to turn philosophy from the study of nature to speculations upon life, but the innovators whom I oppose are turning off attention from life to nature. They seem to think that we are placed here to watch the growth of plants, or the motions of the stars. Socrates was rather of opinion that what we had to learn was, how to do good and avoid evil. —[243]

Benjamin Jowett

⊢ 1817—1893 *English educator and Greek scholar*

Doubt comes in at the window when inquiry is denied at the door.

11 K

Horace Meyer Kallen

⊢ 1882—1974 *German-American philosopher*

Philosophy has fallen into the position of a toper whose first drink was taken to save his life and who ever after lived to drink. —[138]: 22

Immanuel Kant

⊢ 1724—1804 *German philosopher*

We do not need science and philosophy to know what we should do to be honest and good, yea, even wise and virtuous. —[139]

Human reason, in one sphere of its cognition, is called upon to consider questions, which it cannot decline, as they are presented by its own nature, but which it cannot answer, as they transcend every faculty of the mind. —[139]: Preface

John Keats

⊢ 1795—1821 *English poet*

Do not all charms fly
At the mere touch of cold philosophy?
There was an awful rainbow once in heaven:
We know her woof, her texture; she is given
In the dull catalogue of common things.
Philosophy will clip an Angel's wings,
Conquer all mysteries by rule and line,
Empty the haunted air, and gnomed mine–
Unweave a rainbow, ...
—[140]: Part II

John F. Kennedy

⊢ 1917—1963 *American president*

We are not afraid to entrust the American people with unpleasant facts, foreign ideas, alien philosophies, and competitive values. For a nation that is afraid to let its people judge the truth and falsehood in an open market is a nation that is afraid of its people.

Johannes Kepler

⊢ 1571—1630   *German astronomer*

I demonstrate by means of philosophy that the earth is round, and is inhabited on all sides; that it is insignificantly small, and is borne through the stars. —[141]

A warning to sundry Theologos, Medicos and Philosophos, in particular D. Philippus Feselius, that they should not, in their just repudiation of star-gazing superstition, throw out the child with the bath and thus unknowingly act in contradiction to their profession. —[137]: 180

In theology we must consider the predominance of authority; in philosophy the predominance of reason. —[141]

The diversity of the phenomena of nature is so great, and the treasures hidden in the heavens so rich, precisely in order that the human mind shall never be lacking in fresh nourishment.

Charles F. Kettering

⊢ 1876—1958   *American educator*

It is easy to build a philosophy ... it doesn't have to run. —[27]

Dick Keyes

⊢ *American writer*

Relativism says it is impossible to be wrong in any way that matters. As such it is the opiate of the people. —[142]

Søren Aabye Kierkegaard

⊢ 1813—1855 *Danish philosopher*

Philosophy is perfectly right in saying that life must be understood backward. But then one forgets the other clause—that it must be lived forward. —[146]

Philosophy always requires something more, requires the eternal, the true, in contrast to which even the fullest existence as such is but a happy moment. —[144]

At every step philosophy sloughs a skin into a creep its worthless hangers-on. —[143]

What philosophers say about Reality is often as disappointing as a sign you see in a shop window which reads: Pressing Done Here. If you brought your clothes to be pressed, you would be fooled; for only the sign is for sale. —[145]

In relation to their philosophical systems, most philosophers are like a man who builds an enormous castle and lives in a shack close by.

Joseph Wood Krutch

⊢ 1893—1970 *American conservationist and writer*

Logic is the art of going wrong with confidence. —[147]

George Lakoff

⊢ *American psychologist*

It is still widely assumed that the philosophy of mind can be done without empirical research as an armchair pursuit in which Reason reflects directly on the structure of the mind. —[148]: 397

Dalai Lama

⊢ 1935— *Tibetian spiritual leader*

This is my simple religion. There is no need for temples; no need for complicated philosophy. Our own brain, our own heart is our temple; the philosophy is kindness.

Walter Savage Landor

⊢ 1775—1864 *English poet and writer*

All schools of philosophy, and almost all authors, are rather to be frequented for exercise than for weight. —[149]

Suzanne K. Langer

⊢ 1895—1985 *American philosopher*

A philosophy is characterized more by the formulation of its problems than by its solution of them. —[150]

Reprinted by permission of the publisher from PHILOSOPHY IN A NEW KEY: A STUDY IN THE SYMBOLISM OF REASON, RITE, AND ART by Susanne K. Langer, Cambridge, Mass.: Harvard University Press, Copyright © renewed 1942, 1951, 1957 by the President and Fellows of Harvard College, Copyright © renewed 1970, 1979 by Susanne K. Langer, 1985 by Leonard C.R. Langer.

Timothy Leary

⊢ 1920—1996 *American educator*

In the information age, you don't teach philosophy as they did after feudalism. You perform it. If Aristotle were alive today he'd have a talk show. —[155]

Henri Lebesgue

⊢ 1875—1941 *French mathematician*

In my opinion, a mathematician, in so far as he is a mathematician, need not preoccupy himself with philosophy—an opinion, moreover, which has been expressed by many philosophers.
—[156]: 129

Emmanuel Levinas

⊢ 1906—1995 *French philosopher*

If philosophizing consists in assuring oneself of an absolute origin, the philosopher will have to efface the trace of his own footsteps and unendingly efface the traces of the effacing of the traces, in an interminable movement staying where it is.
—[152]: 20

Philosophy is inseperable from skepticism, which follows it like a shadow that it chases away by refuting it, only to find it once again under its feet.—[152]: 168

The best thing about philosophy is that it fails. —[151]: 63

George Henry Lewes

⊢ 1817—1878 *English critic and author*

The true function of philosophy is to educate us in the principles of reasoning and not to put an end to further reasoning by the introduction of fixed conclusions. —[153]

Clive Staples Lewis

⊢ 1898—1963 *Irish philosopher*

Friendship is not necessary, like philosophy, like art. ... It has no survival value; rather it is one of those things that gives value to survival. —[154]

Georg C. Lichtenberg

⊢ 1742—1799 *German aphorist*

Put it how you will, philosophy is only the art of discrimination. The country bumpkin makes use of all the principles of philosophy, though indirectly, latently, or in combination, as the physicist and chemist would say; the philosopher gives us them pure. —[157]: 78

Walter Lippmann

⊢ 1889—1974   *American editor and critic*

When philosophers try to be politicians they generally cease to be philosophers. —[158]: Ch. 3

Thomas Babington Macaulay

⊢ 1800—1859 *English historian and author*

With respect to the doctrine of a future life, a North American Indian knows just as much as any ancient or modern philosopher. —[109]

Logicians may reason about abstractions. But the great mass of men must have images. The strong tendency of the multitude in all ages and nations to idolatry can be explained on no other principle. —[159]

J.L. Mackie

⊢ 1917—1981 *Australian philosopher*

'Slapdash egoism', Midgley says, is not really a very puzzling phenomenon. Nor, I suppose, is slapdash discussion (even in a reputable philosophical journal); but it is deplorable. —[161]

Michael Maier

⊢ 17th Century *Czeck alchemist and physician*

From a man and a woman make a circle, then a square, then a triangle, finally a circle and you will obtain the Philosophers' Stone. —[68]: 123

Joseph De Maistre

⊢ 1753—1821 *French theorist and writer*

There is no philosophy without the art of ignoring objections. —[162]

Emma Martin

⊢ 1812—1850 *English socialist, feminist, and free-thinker*

Religion, with an upward glancing eye, asks what there is above. Philosophy looks around her and seeks to make a happy home of earth. Religion asks what God would have her do: –Philosophy, what nature's laws advise. Religion has never given us laws in which cruelty and vice may not be seen, but philosophy's pure moral code may be thus briefly stated: –'Happiness is the great object of human existence ...' —[96]

Reprinted with the kind permission of Freedom from Religion Foundation, Inc. / Annie Laurie Gaylor.

Karl Marx

⊢ 1818—1883 *German ideologist*

The Philosophers have only interpreted the world in various ways; the point however, is to change it. —[166]

Philosophy stands in the same relation to the study of the actual world as masturbation to sexual love. —[166]

Reason has always existed, only not always in reasonable form. —[165]

W. Somerset Maugham

⊢ 1874—1965 *English novelist and playwright*

The philosopher is like a mountaineer who has with difficulty climbed a mountain for the sake of the sunrise, and arriving at the top finds only fog; whereupon he wanders down again. He must be an honest man if he doesn't tell you that the spectacle was stupendous.

James Clerk Maxwell

⊢ 1831—1871 *English physicist*

If we are ever to discover the laws of nature, we must do so by obtaining the most accurate acquaintance with the facts of nature, and not by dressing up in philosophical language the loose opinions of men who had no knowledge of the facts which throw most light on these laws. And as for those who introduce ethereal or other media to account for these actions, without any direct evidence of the existence of such media, or any clear understanding of how the media do their work, and who fill all space three and four times over with aethers of different sorts, why the less these men talk about their philosophical scruples about admitting action at a distance the better. —[254]

Lou Marinoff

⊢ *American philosopher*

America is Rome reincarnate. Like the Roman empire, the American empire is vastly powerful and unfathomably corrupt. Like Rome, America imposes her civilisation upon an ungrateful world. Like Rome, America needs bread, circuses and philosopher-statesmen to forestall and yet to hasten her demise. —[163]

The 'dark side' of philosophy is compassed both by what it has failed to do in defence and preservation of its own mission—the love of wisdom—and by what this failure has permitted the enemies of open and reasoned inquiry to entrench in its place—the worship of folly. —[164]

James McCosh

⊢ 1811—1894 *Scottish philosopher*

It should be freely admitted that the Scottish school has not discovered all truth, nor even all discoverable truth, in philosophy; that it does not pretend to have done so is one of its excellencies, proceeding from the propriety of its method and the modesty of its character. —[167]

All the great masters of the school not only admit, but are at pains to show, that there are mysteries in the mind of man, and in every department of human speculation, which they cannot clear up. This feature has tempted some to speak of the whole school with contempt, as doing little because attempting little. —[167]

Let it be their claim, that if they have not discovered all truth, they have discovered and settled some truth—while they have not promulgated much error, or wasted their strength in rearing showy fabrics, admired in one age and taken down the next. —[167]

Peter Brian Medawar

⊢ 1915—1987 *English zoologist*

Medical scientists use the word 'iatrogenic' to refer to disabilities that are the consequence of medical treatment. We believe that some such word might be coined to refer to philosophical difficulties for which philosophers themselves are responsible. —[168]: 244

Reprinted by permission of the publisher from ARISTOTLE TO ZOOS: A PHILOSOPHICAL DICTIONARY OF BIOLOGY by P.B. Medawar and J.S. Medawar, Cambridge, Mass.: Harvard University Press, Copyright © 1983 by P.B. Medawar and J.S. Medawar.

H.L. Mencken

⊢ 1880—1956 *American journalist, editor, and essayist*

Philosophy consists very largely of one philosopher arguing that all others are jackasses. He usually proves it, and I should add that he also usually proves that he is one himself. —[169]

Metaphysics is almost always an attempt to prove the incredible by an appeal to the unintelligible. —[169]

... no man of genuinely superior intelligence has ever been an actor. Even supposing a young man of appreciable mental powers to be lured upon the stage, as philosophers are occasionally lured into bordellos, his mind would be inevitably and almost immediately destroyed by the gaudy nonsense issuing from his mouth every night. —[169]

Medicine never really got anywhere until it threw metaphysics overboard. Find me a medical man who still toys with it, and I'll show you a quack. He may be, perhaps, what is called an ethical quack, but he is still a quack. —[169]

Mary Midgley

⊢ 1919— *American philosopher*

If you're doing philosophy at all, if you're engaged in the way that ideas work, then it's a male peculiarity to wish to go right up in the air and go round in circles without relating them to anything else. —[170]

Morally as well as physically, there is only one world, and we all have to live in it.

Robert A. Millikan

⊢ 1868—1953 *American physicist*

Fullness of knowledge always means some understanding of the depths of our ignorance; and that is always conducive to humility and reverence.

John Milton

⊢ 1608—1674 *English poet*

That stone, ... Philosophers in vain so long have sought.
—[171]: bk. III, l. 600

Michel de Montaigne

⊢ 1533—1592 *French philosopher*

It is a thousand pities that matters should be at such a pass in this age of ours, that philosophy, even with men of understanding, should be looked upon as a vain and fantastic name, a thing of no use, no value, either in opinion or effect, of which I think those ergotisms and petty sophistries, by prepossessing the avenues to it, are the cause. And people are much to blame to represent it to children for a thing of so difficult access, and with such a frowning, grim, and formidable aspect. Who is it that has disguised it thus, with this false, pale, and ghostly countenance? There is nothing more airy, more gay, more frolic, and

I had like to have said, more wanton. She preaches nothing but feasting and jollity; a melancholic anxious look shows that she does not inhabit there. —[172]: Of the Education of Children

And what all philosophy cannot implant in the head of the wisest men, does not custom by her sole ordinance teach the crudest common herd? —[172]: Of Custom

Cicero says that to philosophize is nothing else but to prepare for death. This is because study and contemplation draw our soul out of us to some extent and keep it busy outside the body; which is a sort of apprenticeship and semblance of death. Or else it is because all the wisdom and reasoning in the world boils down finally to this point: to teach us not to be afraid to die. —[172]

Hans J. Morgenthau

⊢ 1904—1953   *German-American political scientist*

Propaganda replaces moral philosophy.

Herbert J. Muller

⊢ 1905—1980   *American historian and educator*

Science remains the author of our major problem, in its gift of tremendous power that has been terribly abused; but for the wise use of this power we need more, not less, of the objective dispassionate scientific spirit. For our philosophical purposes we need more of its integrity and its basic humility, its respect at once for the fact and the mystery. —[173]

Iris Murdoch

⊢ 1919—1999   *English writer and university lecturer*

Philosophy! Empty thinking by ignorant conceited men who think they can digest without eating! —[174]: pt. 1

In philosophy, if you aren't moving at a snail's pace you aren't moving at all. —[175]

John Henry Newman

⊢ 1801—1890 *English cardinal*

A great memory does not make a philosopher, any more than a dictionary can be called a grammar. —[176]

Isaac Newton

⊢ 1642—1727 *English physicist*

I intend, to be no further solicitous about matters of Philosophy; and therefore I hope you will not take it ill, if you find me never doing anything more in that kind. —[177]

Physics, beware of metaphysics. —[160]

I know not how I seem to others, but to myself I am but a small child wandering upon the vast shores of knowledge, every now and then finding a small bright pebble to content myself with while the vast ocean of undiscovered truth lay before me.

I shall not mingle conjectures with certainties.

That one body may act upon another at a distance through a vacuum, without the mediation of anything else by and through which their action may be conveyed from one to another, is to me so great an absurdity that I believe no man, who has in philosophical matters a competent faculty of thinking, can ever fall into it.

Friedrich Nietzsche

⊢ 1844—1900   *German philosopher*

How I understand the philosopher—as a terrible explosive, endangering everything ... my concept of the philosopher is worlds removed from any concept that would include even a Kant, not to speak of academic 'ruminants' and other professors of philosophy ... —[182]

If philosophy ever manifested itself as helpful, redeeming, or prophylactic, it was in a healthy culture. The sick, it made even sicker. —[184]

From the book Nietzsche, F. PHILOSOPHY IN THE TRAGIC AGE OF THE GREEKS. Translation by M. Cowan. Copyright 1962, reprinted 1996 by Regnery Publishing, Inc. All rights reserved. Reprinted by special permission of Regnery Publishing Inc., Washington, D.C.

Philosophy leaps ahead on tiny toe-holds; hope and intuition lend wings to its feet. Calculating reason lumbers heavily behind, looking for better footholds, for reason too wants to reach that alluring goal which its divine comrade has long since reached. —[184]

From the book Nietzsche, F. PHILOSOPHY IN THE TRAGIC AGE OF THE GREEKS. Translation by M. Cowan. Copyright 1962, reprinted 1996 by Regnery Publishing, Inc. All rights reserved. Reprinted by special permission of Regnery Publishing Inc., Washington, D.C.

Everything the philosopher asserts about man is basically no more than a statement about man within a very limited time span. A lack of historical sense is the congenital defect of all philosophers. —[183]

Wisdom is a screen behind which the philosopher saves himself because he has become weary, old, cold, hard—as a premonition that the end is near, like the prudence animals have before they die: they go off by themselves, become still, choose solitude, hide in caves, and become wise. —[178]

Gradually it has become clear to me what every great philosophy so far has been: namely, the personal confession of its author and a kind of involuntary and unconscious memoir; also that the moral (or immoral) intentions in every philosophy constituted the real germ of life from which the whole plant has grown. —[180]

To live alone one must be a beast or a god, says Aristotle. Leaving out the third case: one must be both—a philosopher. —[181]

Novalis—Friedrich Freiherr von Hardenberg

⊢   1772—1801   *German poet*

Philosophy is at bottom homesickness—the longing to be at home everywhere. —[185]

Precisely because we are philosophers we need not bother ourselves about issues. We have the principle, that is enough; the rest can be left for the commoner brains. —[185]

Robert Nozick

⊢ 1938—2002 *American philosopher*

Why are philosophers intent on forcing others to believe things. Is that a nice way to behave towards someone? —[186]

Reprinted by permission of the publisher from PHILOSOPHICAL EXPLANATIONS by Robert Nozick, Cambridge, Mass.: The Belknap Press of Harvard University Press, Copyright © 1981 by Robert Nozick.

Michael Oakeshott

⊢ 1901—1992 *English philosopher of history*

Anyone who has had a glimpse of the range and subtlety of the thought of Plato or of Hegel will long ago have despaired of becoming a philosopher. —[187]

Julius Robert Oppenheimer

⊢ 1904—1967 *American physicist*

Today, it is not only that our kings do not know mathematics, but our philosophers do not know mathematics and – to go a step further – our mathematicians do not know mathematics. —[188]: 217

The true scientist never loses the faculty of amusement. It is the essence of his being.

Origen

⊢ 185—253 *Alexandrian philosopher*

The highest good, then, after the attainment of which the whole of rational nature is seeking, which is also called the end of all blessings, is defined by many philosophers as follows: The highest good, they say, is to become as like to God as possible. —[189]

P.D. Ouspensky

⊢ 1878—1947 *Russian author, thinker, and mystic*

Or, which is still worse, philosophy is nothing but self-satisfied dialectic surrounding itself with impenetrable barrier of terminology unintelligible to the uninitiated and solving for itself all the problems of the universe without any possibility of proving these explanations or making them unintelligible to ordinary mortals. —[190]: 25

16

Philippus Aureolus Paracelsus

⊢ 1493—1541 *German physician, chemist, and alchemist*

Poor Aristotle, he was an acute dreamer. He adduced his arguments in a reasonable, eloquent and entertaining way, and how wonderful it would be if Nature behaved as orderly as Aristotle's inferences. —[192]

What is Aristotle other than fantasy? And in your schools you can nothing but read, and when it is not written you can do nothing. It is none other than speculation, what humans invent by their own powers. —[192]

Regardless of how the philosophy of Aristotle and Albert the Great is described who will believe liars? They do not talk of natural philosophy but of fantasy. They never understood Nature from which you shall learn; Thomas Aquinas and Aristotle and Avicenna have no other reason than empty speculation. —[192]

Cyril Northcote Parkinson

⊢ 1642—1727 *English historian and writer*

The Law of Triviality:
Briefly stated, it means that the time spent on any item of the agenda will be in inverse proportion to the sum of the involved.
—[193]

David Papineau

⊢ 1947— *English philosopher*

I worry about the worth of philosophy done by philosophers who have been trained in nothing else. —[191]

Blaise Pascal

⊢ 1623—1662 *French mathematician, physicist, and religious philosopher*

To ridicule philosophy is really to philosophize.
—[194]: No. 430

To have no time for [or, not to care for] philosophy is to be a true philosopher. —[194]: No. 513

I cannot forgive Descartes; in all his philosophy he did his best to dispense with God. But he could not avoid making Him set

the world in motion with a flip of His thumb; after that he had
no more use for God. —[194]: No. 513

Boris L. Pasternak

⊢ 1890—1960   *Russian writer*

That's metaphysics, my dear fellow. It's forbidden me by my
doctor, my stomach won't take it. —[195]: Ch. 1, sect. 5

Charles Peguy

⊢ 1873—1914   *French author*

A great philosophy is not one that passes final judgments and
establishes ultimate truth. It is one that causes uneasiness and
starts commotion.

Charles S. Peirce

⊢ 1839—1914   *American logician, philosopher, and scientist*

Let us not pretend to doubt in philosophy what we do not doubt
in our hearts. —[196]

The truth is, that common sense, or thought as it first emerges
above the level of the narrowly practical, is deeply imbued with

that bad logical quality to which the epithet metaphysical is commonly applied; and nothing can clear it up but a severe course of logic. —[196]

Few persons care to study logic, because everybody conceives himself to be proficient enough in the art of reasoning already. But I observe that this satisfaction is limited to one's own ratiocination, and does not extend to that of other men. —[196]

Upon this first, an in one sense this sole, rule of reason, that in order to learn you must desire to learn, and in so desiring not be satisfied with what you already incline to think, there follows one corollary, which itself deserves to be inscribed upon every wall in the city of philosophy: Do not block the way of inquiry. —[218]

The pragmatist knows that doubt is an art which has to be acquired with difficulty. —[196]

It ... is easy to be certain. One has only to be sufficiently vague. —[196]

Albert Pike

⊢ 1809—1891 *American general*

Philosophy is a kind of journey, ever learning yet never arriving at the ideal perfection of truth. —[198]

Robert M. Pirsig

⊢ 1928— *American philosopher*

Metaphysics is a restaurant where they give you a thirty thousand page menu, and no food. —[199]

Extract from ZEN AND THE ART OF MOTORCYCLE MAINTENANCE by Robert Pirsig published by Bodley Head. Used by permission of the Random House Group Limited.

Max Planck

⊢ 1858—1947 *German physicist*

A new scientific truth does not triumph by convincing its opponents and making them see the light but rather because its opponents eventually die and a new generation grows up that is familiar with it. —[200]

Science cannot solve the ultimate mystery of nature. And that is because, in the last analysis, we ourselves are part of nature and therefore part of the mystery that we are trying to solve. —[200]

Plotinus

⊢ 204—270   *Greek philosopher*

The musician we may think of as being exceedingly quick to beauty, drawn in a very rapture to it: somewhat slow to stir of his own impulse, he answers at once to the outer stimulus: as the timid are sensitive to noise so he to tones and the beauty they convey; all that offends against unison or harmony in melodies and rhythms repels him; he longs for measure and shapely pattern. —[202]

The born lover, to whose degree the musician also may attain – and then either come to a stand or pass beyond – has a certain memory of beauty but, severed from it now, he no longer comprehends it: spellbound by visible loveliness he clings amazed about that. His lesson must be to fall down no longer in bewildered delight before some, one embodied form. —[202]

The metaphysician, equipped by that very character, winged already and not like those others, in need of disengagement, stirring of himself towards the supernal but doubting of the way, needs only a guide. He must be shown, then, and instructed, a willing wayfarer by his very temperament, all but self-directed. —[202]

Plutarch

⊢ 45—125   *Greek philosopher*

When Eudæmonidas heard a philosopher arguing that only a wise man can be a good general, This is a wonderful speech, said he; but he that saith it never heard the sound of trumpets. —[203]

There are two sentences inscribed upon the Ancient oracle ... 'Know thyself' and 'Nothing too much'; and upon these all other precepts depend. —[203]

Henri Poincaré

⊢ 1854—1912   *French mathematician and philosopher of science*

To doubt everything or to believe everything are two equally convenient solutions; both dispense with the necessity of reflection. —[204]

Science is built up of facts, as a house is built of stones; but an accumulation of facts is no more a science than a heap of stones is a house. —[204]

Sociology is the science with the greatest number of methods and the least results. —[204]

Michael Polanyi

⊢ 1891—1976   *Hungarian scientist turned philosopher*

Modern science disclaims any intention of understanding the hidden nature of things; its philosophy condemns any such endeavour as vague, misleading and altogether unscientific ... . But I refuse to heed this warning. I agree that the process of understanding leads beyond – indeed far beyond – what a strict empiricism regards as the domain of legitimate knowledge; but I reject such an empiricism. If consistently applied, it would discredit any knowledge whatever and it can be upheld only by allowing it to remain inconsistent. It is permitted this inconsistency because its ruthless mutilation of human experience lends it such a high reputation for scientific severity, that its prestige overrides the defensiveness of its own foundations. Our acknowledgement of understanding as a valid form of knowing will go a long way towards liberating our minds from this violent and inefficient despotism. —[205]

Terrence Pratchett

⊢ 1948— *English writer*

His philosophy was a mixture of three famous schools: the Cynics, the Stoics and the Epicureans—and summed up all three of them in his famous phrase, 'You can't trust any bugger further than you can throw him, and there's nothing you can do about it, so let's have a drink.' —[207]

J.J. Procter

⊢ 1888—1955

The child's philosophy is a true one. He does not despise the bubble because it bursts; and he immediately sets to work to blow another one. —[219]

Hilary Putnam

⊢ 1926— *American logician and philosopher*

The incoherence of the attempts to turn the world views of either physics or history into secular theologies have not yet been entirely exposed, but the process is, I hope, well under way. As philosophers, we seem caught between our desire for integration and our recognition of the difficulty. I don't know what the solution to this tension will look like. But Etienne Gilson was right when he wrote that 'Philosophy always buries its undertakers.' —[209]: 303

I think part of the appeal of mathematical logic is that the formulas look mysterious—You write backward Es! —[210]

17   Q

Queen Victoria

⊢ 1819—1910   *English queen*

I would earnestly warn you against trying to find out the reason for and explanation of everything ... To try and find out the reason for everything is very dangerous and leads to nothing but disappointment and dissatisfaction, unsettling your mind and in the end making you miserable. —[211]

Willard v. Quine

⊢ 1908—2000   *American logician and philosopher*

I see philosophy not as an *a priori* propaedeutic or groundwork for science, but as continuous with science. I see philosophy and science as in the same boat—a boat which, to revert to Neurath's figure as I so often do, we can rebuild only at sea while staying afloat in it. There is no external vantage point, no first philosophy. —[213]: 126

To be is to be that value of a variable. There are no ultimate philosophical problems concerning terms and their references, but only concerning variables and their values; and there are no ultimate philosophical problems concerning existence except insofar as existence is expressed by the quantifier '$\exists x$'. —[215]: 224

Reprinted by permission of the publisher from METHODS OF LOGIC by W.v. Quine, Cambridge, Mass.: Harvard University Press, Copyright © 1950, 1959, 1972, 1978, 1982 by W.v.Quine.

The philosopher's task differs from the others', then, in detail; but in no such drastic way as those suppose who imagine for the philosopher a vantage point outside the conceptual scheme that he takes in charge. There is no such cosmic exile. He cannot study and revise the fundamental conceptual scheme of science and common sense without having some conceptual scheme, whether the same or another no less in need of philosophical scrutiny, in which to work. —[212]

Physics investigates the essential nature of the world, and biology describes a local bump. Psychology, human psychology, describes a bump on a bump. —[214]

Reprinted by the kind permission of Douglas B. Quine.

Anthony Quinton

⊢ 1925— *English philosopher*

Nowadays there are no serious philosophers who are not looking forward to the pension to which their involvement with the subject entitles them. —[216]

18   R

Frank Ramsey

⊢ 1903—1930   *English logician and philosopher*

The chief danger to our philosophy, apart from laziness and wooliness, is *scholaticism*, the essence of which is treating what is vague as if it were precise and trying to fit it into an exact logical category. —[217]: 269

Ayn Rand

⊢ 1905—1982   *Russian-American writer*

The battle of philosophers is a battle for man's mind. If you don't understand their theories, you are vulnerable to the worst among them.

W. Winwood Reade

⊢ 1838—1875   *English poet*

The philosophic spirit of inquiry may be traced to brute curiosity, and that to the habit of examining all things in search of food. —[220]: Ch. 3

Thomas Reid

⊢ 1710—1796   *English philosopher*

It is genius, and not the want of it, that adulterates philosophy, and fills it with error and false theory. —[221]: 99

Suppose that such a man [a plain one] meets with a modern philosopher, and wants to be informed what smell in plant is. The philosopher tells him that there is no smell in plants, nor in anything but the mind; that it is impossible there can be smell but in a mind; and that all this hath been demonstrated by modern philosophy. The plain man will, no doubt, be apt to think him merry. —[221]: 112

To what purpose is it for philosophy to decide common sense in this or any other matter? The belief of a material world is older, and of more authority, than any principles of philosophy. It declines the tribunal of reason, and laughs of all the artillery of the logician. —[221]: 127

If a philosopher should undertake to account for the force of gunpowder in the discharge of a musket, and then tell us that the cause of this phenomenon is the drawing of the trigger, we should not be much wiser by this account. —[221]: 354

Nicolas Rescher

⊢ 1928— *American philosopher*

In philosophy we ... cannot rise above the battles of the schools. The proliferation of points of view is inherent in the enterprise. We cannot attain a 'position of reason' outside the arena of controversy. —[222]

From THE STRIFE OF SYSTEMS by Nicolas Rescher, © 1985 by University of Pittsburgh Press. Reprinted by permission of the University of Pittsburgh Press.

Charles Richter

⊢ 1900—1985 *American seismologist*

According to Democritus, truth lies at the bottom of a well, the water of which serves as a mirror in which objects may be reflected. I have heard, however, that some philosophers, in seeking for truth, to pay homage to her, have seen their own image and adored it instead.

Francois De La Rochefoucauld

⊢ 1613—1680 *French classical author*

Philosophy triumphs easily over past evils and future evils; but present evils triumph over it. —[223]

The strongest symptom of wisdom in man is his being sensible of his own follies. —[223]

Jean Jacques Rousseau

⊢ 1712—1778   *French philosopher*

I also realized that the philosophers, far from ridding me of my vain doubts, only multiplied the doubts that tormented me and failed to remove any one of them. So I chose another guide and said, Let me follow the Inner Light; it will not lead me so far astray as others have done, or if it does it will be my own fault, and I shall not go so far wrong if I follow my own illusions as if I trusted to their deceits. —[228]

Richard Rorty

⊢ 1931—   *American philosopher*

The philosophers' own little definitions of 'philosophy' are merely polemical devices—intended to exclude from the field of honor those whose pedigrees are unfamiliar. We can pick out 'the philosophers' in the contemporary intellectual world only by noting who is commenting on a certain sequence of historical figures. All that 'philosophy' as a name for a sector of culture means is 'talk about Plato, Augustine, Descartes, Kant, Hegel, Frege, Russell ... and that lot.' Philosophy is best seen as a kind of writing. It is delimited, as any literary genre, not by form or matter, but by tradition—a familiar romance involving e.g., Father Parmenides, honest old Uncle Kant, and bad brother Derrida. —[225]

One of the benefits of getting rid of the notion of the intrinsic nature of reality is that you get rid of the notion that quarks and human rights differ in 'ontological status'. This, in turn, helps you reject the suggestion that natural science should serve as a paradigm for the rest of culture, and in particular that philosophical progress consists in philosophers getting more scientific. —[226]

Reprinted by the kind permission of University of Minnesota Press.

A lot of people now find belief in God immature, and eventually a lot of people may find realism immature. —[227]

Bertrand Russell

⊢ 1872—1970   *English mathematician and philosopher*

I think that bad philosophers may have a certain influence, good philosophers, never. —[230]

Organic life, we are told, has developed gradually from the protozoon to the philosopher and this development, we are assured is indubitably in advance. Unfortunately it is the philosopher, not the protozoon, who gives us this assurance.

Philosophy is an unusually ingenious attempt to think fallaciously.

The point of philosophy is to start with something so simple as not to seem worth stating, and to end with something so paradoxical that no one will believe it.
—[231]: The Philosophy of Logical Atomism

In very abstract studies such as philosophical logic, ... the subject-matter that you are supposed to be thinking of is so exceedingly difficult and elusive that any person who has ever

tried to think about it knows you do not think about it except perhaps once in six months for half a minute. The rest of the time you think about the symbols, because they are tangible, for the thing you are supposed to be thinking about is fearfully difficult and one does not often manage to think about it. The really good philosopher is the one who does once in six months think about it for a minute. Bad philosophers never do.
—[231]: The Philosophy of Logical Atomism

Aristotle maintained that women have fewer teeth than men; although he was twice married, it never occurred to him to verify this statement by examining his wives' mouths.
—[229]: An Outline of Intellectual Rubbish

[On philosophy] Should be piecemeal and provisional like science; final truth belongs to heaven, not to this world.

The essential characteristic of philosophy which makes it a study distinct from science, is *criticism*. It examines critically the principles employed in science and in daily life; it searches out any inconsistencies there may be in these principles, and it only accepts them when, as the result of a critical inquiry, no reason for rejecting them has appeared. —[235]

Optimism and pessimism, as cosmic philosophies, show the same naive humanism; the great world, so far as we know it from the philosophy of nature, is neither good nor bad, and is not concerned to make us happy or unhappy. —[233]

[W]hen people begin to philosophize they seem to think it necessary to make themselves artificially stupid. —[234]

Science is what you know, philosophy is what you don't know.

The collection of prejudices which is called political philosophy is useful provided that it is not called philosophy. —[232]

The process of sound philosophizing, to my mind, consists mainly in passing from those obvious, vague, ambiguous things, that we feel quite sure of, to something precise, clear, definite, which by reflection and analysis we find is involved in the vague thing that we start from, and is, so to speak, the real truth of which that vague thing is a sort of shadow. —[231]: 179

I once received a letter from an eminent logician, Mrs. Christine Ladd Franklin, saying that she was a solipsist, and was surprised that there were no others. Coming from a logician this surprise surprised me. —[232]

Gilbert Ryle

⊢ 1900—1976   *English philosopher*

Soo too Plato was, in my view, a very unreliable Platonist. He was too much of a philosopher to think that anything he had said was the last word. It was left to the disciples to identify his footmarks with his destination. —[236]: Ch. 1

Philosophy is the replacement of category-habits by category-disciplines. —[237]: Introduction

19   S

Marquis de Sade

⊢ 1740—1814 *French writer*

The ultimate triumph of philosophy would be to cast light upon the mysterious ways in which Providence moves to achieve the designs it has for man. —[239]

They declaim against the passions without bothering to think that it is from their flame philosophy lights its torch. —[238]: Pt. 1

Carl Sagan

⊢ 1934—1996 *American astronomer and educator*

Philosophers and scientists confidently offer up traits said to be uniquely human, and the monkeys and apes casually knock them down—toppling the pretension that humans constitute some sort of biological aristocracy among the beings on Earth.

There is something stunningly narrow about how the Anthropic Principal is phrased. Yes, only certain laws and constants of nature are consistent with our kind of life. But essentially the same laws and constants are required to make a rock. So why not talk about a Universe designed so rocks could one day come to be, and strong and weak Lithic Principals? If stones could philosophize, I imagine Lithic Principals would be at the intellectual frontiers.

Seigneur de Saint-Evremond

⊢   1610—1703   *French writer*

Too austere a philosophy makes few wise men; too rigorous politics, few good subjects; too hard a religion, few persons whose devotion is of long continuance.

George Santayana

⊢   1863—1952   *American philosopher*

The empiricist ... thinks he believes only what he sees, but he is much better at believing than seeing. —[240]

Viewed from a sufficient distance, all systems of philosophy are seen to be personal, temperamental, accidental and premature. —[240]

Scepticism is the chastity of the intellect, and it is shameful to surrender it too soon or to the first comer. —[240]

Jean Paul Sartre

⊢ 1905—1980   *French philosopher*

If I became a philosopher, if I have so keenly sought this fame for which I'm still waiting, it's all been to seduce women basically.

Like all dreamers, I mistook disenchantment for truth.

Friedrich von Schlegel

⊢ 1772—1829   *German philosopher*

As yet every great philosopher has explained his predecessors – often quite unintentionally – in such a way that it seemed that before him they had been entirely misunderstood. —[242]

Reprinted by the kind permission of University of Minnesota Press.

The fact that one can annihilate a philosophy ... or that one can prove that a philosophy annihilates itself is of little consequence. If it's really philosophy, then, like a phoenix, it will always rise again from its own ashes. —[242]

Reprinted by the kind permission of University of Minnesota Press.

Friedrich Schleirmacher

⊢ 1768—1834   *German philosopher*

Knowing the world means knowing that one doesn't signify much in it, means believing that no philosophical dream can be realized in it, and means hoping that it will never be otherwise, or at best only somewhat flimsier. —[242]: 217

Arthur Schopenhauer

⊢ 1788—1860   *German philosopher*

Should you ever intend to dull the wits of a young man and to incapacitate his brains for any kind of thought whatever, then you cannot do better than give him Hegel to read.
—[206]: 2.12.5(f)

Governments make of philosophy a means of serving their state interests, and scholars make of it a trade. —[206]: 2.12.1

Charles Schulz

⊢ 1922—2000   *American illustrator*

There's a difference between a philosophy and a bumper sticker.

John Selden

⊢ 1584—1654 *English writer and politician*

Philosophy is nothing but Discretion. —[244]

William Shakespeare

⊢ 1564—1616 *English playwright*

It goes much against my stomach. Hast any philosophy in thee, shepherd?
—[245]: *As You Like It*, Act iii. Sc. 2.

Adversity's sweet milk, philosophy.
—[245]: *Romeo and Juliet*, Act iii. Sc. 3.

For there was never yet philosopher That could endure the toothache patiently.
—[245]: *Much Ado about Nothing*, Act v. Sc. 1.

There are more things in heaven and earth, Horatio, Than are dreamt of in your philosophy.
—[245]: *Hamlet*, Act i. Sc. 5.

George Bernard Shaw

⊢ 1856—1950 *English writer*

The philosopher is Nature's pilot. And there you have our difference; to be in hell is to drift, to be in heaven is to steer. —[247]

The fact that a believer is happier than a skeptic is no more to the point than the fact that a drunken man is happier than a sober one. The happiness of credulity is a cheap and dangerous quality. —[246]: The Doctors Dilemma

A fool's brain digests philosophy into folly, science into superstition, and art into pedantry. Hence University education.

J.J.C. Smart

⊢ 1920— *Australian philosopher*

This characteristic inconclusiveness of philosophical argument is a fact familiar to all philosophers. If they were to take seriously more of them would be favorably disposed to my conception of philosophy as in part depending on merely plausible considerations. If a philosopher keeps on patching up his theory we may try to persuade him that this way of thinking is becoming more and more baroque and is ill-fitting to our scientific knowledge. —[248]: 13

Adam Smith

⊢ 1723—1790 *English economist and philosopher*

The machines that are first invented to perform any particular movement are always the most complex, and succeeding artists generally discover that with fewer wheels, with fewer principles of motion than has originally been employed, the same effects may be more easily produced. The first philosophical systems, in the same manner, are always the most complex. —[249]

George H. Smith

⊢ *American philosopher*

The significant contribution of empiricism was not the eradication of certainty, but the eradication of infallibility as a criterion of certainty. And this shift from infallibilism to fallibilism has profound consequences not only for toleration, but also for the subordination of faith to reason and theology to philosophy. — [250]: 123

Raymond M. Smullyan

⊢ 1919— *American logician, philosopher and magician*

Look, at this point I have become an anti-solipsist, I believe everybody else exist except me.
—[Personal communication]

Socrates

⊢ 470—399 BC   *Greek philosopher*

My advice to you is get married: if you find a good wife you'll be happy; if not, you'll become a philosopher. —[201]

How many things I can do without! —[61]

Herbert Spencer

⊢ 1820—1903   *American philosopher*

How often misused words generate misleading thoughts. —[251]

The ultimate result of shielding men from the effects of folly, is to fill the world with fools. —[251]

When a man's knowledge is not in order, the more of it he has the greater will be his confusion. —[251]

Oswald Spengler

⊢ 1880—1936   *German philosopher*

The mathematics, then, is an art. As such it has its styles and style periods. It is not, as the layman and the philosopher (who is in this matter a layman too) imagine, substantially unalterable, but subject like every art to unnoticed changes from epoch to epoch. The development of the great arts ought never to be treated without an (assuredly not unprofitable) side-glance at contemporary mathematics. —[252]

I maintain that today many an inventor, many a diplomat, many a financier is a sounder philosopher than all those who practice the dull craft of experimental psychology. —[252]

Vilhjálmur Stefánsson

⊢ 1879—1962   *Icelandic-American arctic explorer*

The philosophers of the Middle Ages demonstrated both that the Earth did not exist and also that it was flat. Today they are still arguing about whether the world exists, but they no longer dispute about whether it is flat. —[253]

Gertrude Stein

⊢ 1874—1946   *American writer*

But then of course a philosophy is not the same thing as a style. —[208]

James Stephens

⊢ 1882—1950   *Irish poet and fiction writer*

'Finality is death. Perfection is finality. Nothing is perfect. There are lumps in it,' said the Philosopher. —[255]: Ch. 4

Wallace Stevens

⊢ 1879—1955   *American poet*

The philosopher proves that the philosopher exists. The poet merely enjoys existence. —[257]

Perhaps it is of more value to infuriate philosophers than to go along with them. —[256]

Tom Stoppard

⊢ 1937—   *Czech-English journalist and writer*

Almost everyone who didn't know what to do, did philosophy. Well, that's logical. —[258]

If rationality were the criterion for things being allowed to exist, the world would be one gigantic field of soya beans. —[259]

You talked animatedly for some time about language being the aniseed trail that draws the hounds of heaven when the metaphysical fox has gone to earth; he must have thought you were barmy. —[259]

Harriet Beecher Stowe

⊢ 1811—1896 *American writer and reformer*

Mothers are the most instinctive philosophers. —[260]

P.F. Strawson

⊢ 1919— *English philosopher*

Hence, the appearance of endemic disagreement in the subject is something to be expected rather than deplored; and it is no matter for wonder that the individual philosopher's view are more likely than those of the scientist or exact scholar to reflect in part his individual taste and temperament. —[261]: vii

August Strindberg

⊢ 1849—1912 *Swedish author*

[On philosophy] A history of falsehood.

Adam Swift

⊢ *English philosopher and sociologist*

In refusing to take seriously the feasibility constraints which are the stuff of real politics, philosophers refuse to grow up.
—[262]

What has a philosopher got to do with a politician? One can't do and the other can't think. Time for a third way.

Charles Taylor

⊢ 1931— *Canadian philosopher*

I think that philosophy in most aspects is pretty well useless and hopeless unless it's done with other disciplines. And that's the way I like to do it. —[263]

Alfred Lord Tennyson

⊢ 1809—1892 *English poet*

Hold thou the good;
define it well;
For fear divine Philosophy
Should push beyond her
mark, and be
Procuress to the Lords
of Hell.
—[264]: *In Memoriam*, LIII

James Thomson

⊢ 1700—1748 *English poet and dramatist*

For still the world prevail'd, and its dread laugh,
Which scarce the firm philosopher can scorn.
—[265]: *The Seasons.* 'Autumn', line 233

Henry David Thoreau

⊢ 1817—1862 *American writer and philosopher*

What sort of philosophers are we, who know absolutely nothing about the origin and destiny of cats?

To a philosopher all news, as it is called, is gossip, and they who edit it and read it are old women over their tea.

The broadest philosophy is narrower than the worst poetry.
—[75]

Poetry implies the whole truth, philosophy expresses only a particle of it.

There are now-a-days professors of philosophy but not philosophers. —[266]

To be a philosopher is not merely to have subtle thoughts; but so to love wisdom as to live according to its dictates.

A farmer, a hunter, a soldier, a reporter, even a philosopher, may be daunted; but nothing can deter a poet, for he is actuated by pure love. Who can predict his comings and goings? His business calls him out at all hours, even when doctors sleep. —[266]

We do not learn by inference and deduction and the application of mathematics to philosophy, but by direct intercourse and sympathy.

W.H. Thorpe

⊢ *English zoologist*

Bertrand Russell was giving a lesson on solipsism to a lay audience, and a woman got up and said she was delighted to hear Bertrand Russell say he was a solipsist; she was one too, and she wished there were more of us. —[267]

James Thurber

⊢ 1894—1961   *American writer and cartoonist*

Philosophy offers the rather cold consolation that perhaps we and our planet do not actually exist; religion presents the contradictory and scarcely more comforting thought that we exist but that we cannot hope to get anywhere until we cease to exist. Alcohol, in attempting to resolve the contradiction, produces vivid patterns of Truth which vanish like snow in the morning sun and cannot be recalled; the revelations of poetry are as wonderful as a comet in the skiesand as mysterious. Love, which was once believed to contain the Answer, we now know to be nothing more than an inherited behavior pattern. —[268]

I BELIEVE: THE PERSONAL PHILOSOPHIES OF CERTAIN EMINENT MEN AND WOMEN OF OUR TIME, edited by Clifton Fadirman. This quote printed by arrangement with Rosemary A. Thurber and The Barbara Hogenson Agency, Inc.

Lev Nikolaevich Tolstoi

⊢ 1828—1910   *Russian writer*

It is easier to write ten volumes of philosophy than to put one principle into practice.

Slavery was contrary to all the moral principles advocated by Plato and Aristotle, yet neither of them saw this because to renounce slavery would have meant the collapse of the life they were living. —[269]: 6

Mark Twain

⊢ 1835—1910   *American writer and humorist*

The perfection of wisdom, and the end of true philosophy is to proportion our wants to our possessions, our ambitions to our capacities, we will then be a happy and a virtuous people. —[270]

Stephen Vizinczey

⊢ 1933— *Hungarian-born English writer*

Consistency is a virtue for trains: what we want from a philosopher is insights, whether he comes by them consistently or not. —[272]

Francois Marie Arouet Voltaire

⊢ 1694—1778 *French philosopher and author*

When he to whom one speaks does not understand, and he who speaks himself does not understand, that is metaphysics. —[273]

[On metaphysics] Consists of two parts, first, that which all men of sense already know, and second, that which they can never know. —[273]

[On the philosopher] People who talk about something they don't understand, and make you think its your fault. —[273]

Philosopher: A lover of wisdom, which is to say, Truth. —[273]

[Invited a second time to an orgy]. Ah no, my good friends, once a philosopher, twice a pervert. —[273]

All is for the best in the best of possible worlds. —[273]

Bernard de Voto

⊢ 1897—1955   *American historian, critic, and novelist*

The mind has its own logic but does not often let others in on it.

22

Frans de Waal

⊢ 1948— *Dutch zoologist and ethologist*

I've argued that many of what philosophers call moral sentiments can be seen in other species. In chimpanzees and other animals, you see examples of sympathy, empathy, reciprocity, a willingness to follow social rules. Dogs are a good example of a species that have and obey social rules; that's why we like them so much, even though they're large carnivores. —[271]

Mary Warnock

⊢ 1924— *English philosopher*

I've never known such adversarial people as women philosophers. I certainly don't think that they're little timid creatures that can't speak up in a seminar. Far from it—they sometimes dominate the scene. —[275]

Kevin Warwick

⊢ *English computer scientist*

Shouldn't I join the ranks of academic philosophers and merely make unsubstantiated claims about the wonders of human consciousness? Shouldn't I stop trying to do some science and keep my head down? Indeed not. —[276]

Reprinted by the kind permission of Kevin Warwick.

I feel that we are all philosophers, and that those who describe themselves as a 'philosopher' simply do not have a day job to go to. —[277]: 58

Reprinted by the kind permission of Kevin Warwick.

Alan W. Watts

⊢ 1915—1973 *American philosopher*

A philosopher is a sort of intellectual yokel who gawks at things that sensible people take for granted. —[278]

Simone Weil

⊢ 1909—1943 *French religious philosopher*

The proper method of philosophy consists in clearly conceiving the insoluble problems in all their insolubility and then in simply contemplating them, fixedly and tirelessly, year after year, without any hope, patiently waiting. —[279]

When science, art, literature, and philosophy are simply the manifestation of personality they are on a level where glorious and dazzling achievements are possible, which can make a man's name live for thousands of years. But above this level, far above, separated by an abyss, is the level where the highest things are achieved. These things are essentially anonymous. —[280]

Steven Weinberg

⊢ 1933— *American physicist*

In our hunt for the final theory, physicists are more like hounds than hawks; we have become good at sniffing around on the ground for traces of the beauty we expect in the laws of nature, but we do not seem to be able to see the path to the truth from the heights of philosophy. —[281]

From time to time since then I have tried to read current work on the philosophy of science. Some of it I found to be written in a jargon so impenetrable that I can only think that it aimed at impressing those who confound obscurity with profundity. —[281]

I know of no one who has participated actively in the advance of physics in the postwar period whose research has been significantly helped by the work of philosophers. —[281]

Even where philosophical doctrines have in the past been useful to scientists, they have generally lingered on too long, becoming of more harm than they ever were of use. —[281]

Physicists do of course carry around with them a working philosophy. For most of us, it is a rough-and-ready realism, a belief in the objective reality of the ingredients of our scientific theories. But this has been learned through the experience of scientific research and rarely from the teachings of philosophers. —[281]

Tom Weller

⊢ *American writer*

The Greek philosophers began by asking fundamental questions about the nature of life, the universe, and thought itself. They soon discovered that the answers to these questions were not forthcoming, nor likely to be. —[282]

Alfred N. Whitehead

⊢ 1861—1947 *English mathematician and philosopher*

Philosophy begins in wonder. And, at the end, when philosophic thought has done its best, the wonder remains. —[284]: 3.8

The safest general characterization of the European philosophical tradition is that it consists of a series of footnotes to Plato. —[283]: 2.1.1

How shallow, puny, and imperfect are efforts to sound the depths in the nature of things. In philosophical discussion, the merest hint of dogmatic certainty as to finality of statement is an exhibition of folly. —[283]: Preface

Philosophers have disdained the information about the universe obtained through their visceral feelings, and have concentrated on visual feelings. —[283]: 120

I regret that it has been necessary for me in this lecture to administer a large dose of four-dimensional geometry. I do not apologize, because I am really not responsible for the fact that nature in its most fundamental aspect is four-dimensional. Things are what they are ... —[285]

Among medieval and modern philosophers, anxious to establish the religious significance of God, an unfortunate habit has prevailed of paying to Him metaphysical compliments.

The guiding motto in the life of every natural philosopher should be, Seek simplicity and distrust it. —[285]: 163

Norbert Wiener

⊢ 1894—1964   *American mathematician*

The modern physicist is a quantum theorist on Monday, Wednesday, and Friday and a student of gravitational relativity theory on Tuesday, Thursday, and Saturday. On Sunday he is praying that someone will find the reconciliation between the two views. —[286]

[M]athematics is a field in which one's blunders tend to show very clearly and can be corrected or erased with a stroke of the pencil. —[286]

The more we get out of the world, the less we leave, and in the long run we shall have to pay our debts at a time that may be very inconvenient for our own survival. —[286]

P. Eugene Wigner

⊢ 1902—1995 *Hungarian-American physicist*

[While] solipsism may be logically consistent with present quantum mechanics, monism in the sense of materialism is not. —[288]

The simplicities of natural laws arise through the complexities of the language we use for their expression. —[288]

Somebody once said philosophy is the misuse of terminology which was invented just for this purpose. In the same vein, I would say that mathematics is the science of skillful operations with concepts and rules invented just for this purpose. —[287]

Oscar Wilde

⊢ 1854—1900 *English poet and playwright*

Philosophy teaches us to bear with equanimity the misfortunes of others. —[289]

Truth, in matters of religion, is simply the opinion that has survived. —[289]

Thornton Wilder

⊢ 1897—1975 *American writer*

My advice to you is not to inquire why or whither, but just enjoy your ice-cream while it's on your plate, —that's my philosophy. —[290]

THE SKIN OF OF OUR TEETH by Thornton Wilder, Copyright © 1942 The Wilder Family LCC. Printed by arrangement with The Barbara Hogenson Agency, Inc.

Edward O. Wilson

⊢ *American zoologist*

The scientists, not the philosophers, now address most effectively the great questions of existence, the mind, and the meaning of the human condition. —[295]

Ludwig Wittgenstein

⊢ 1889—1951 *Austrian philosopher*

For a philosopher, there is more grass growing down in the green valleys of silliness than up on the barren heights of cleverness. —[292]: §80

The philosopher's treatment of a question is like the treatment of an illness. —[293]: §235

The solution of philosophical problems can be compared with a gift in a fairy tale: in the magic castle it appears enchanted and if you look at it outside in daylight it is nothing but an ordinary bit of iron (or something of the sort). —[292]: 11

In philosophy the winner of the race is the one who can run most slowly. Or: the one who gets there last.

[On philosophy] Simply puts everything before us and neither explains nor deduces anything.

Philosophy limits the thinkable and therefore the unthinkable.

Philosophy aims at the logical clarification of thoughts. Philosophy is not a body of doctrine but an activity. A philosophical work consists essentially of elucidations. —[294]: §4.112

Philosophy can be said to consist of three activities: to see the common sense answer, to get yourself so deeply into the problem that the common sense answer is unbearable, and to get from that situation back to the common sense answer.
—[291]: 108–109

I'm doing philosophy like an old woman, first I'm looking for my pencil, then I'm looking for my glasses, then I'm looking for my glasses again ...

In philosophy you cannot discover anything. I myself, however, had not clearly enough understood this and offended against it. —[274]: 182

When we do philosophy we are like savages, primitive people, who hear the expressions of civilized men, put a false interpretation on them, and then draw the queerest conclusions from it. —[293]: §194

What is the aim of philosophy?—To show the fly the way out of the flybottle. —[293]: §309

A serious and good philosophical work could be written consisting entirely of jokes.

Philosophy, as we use the word, is a fight against the fascination which forms of expression exert upon us. —[291]

Philosophical illnesses usually stem from a dietary deficiency.

Philosophical problems begin when language goes on holiday. —[293]

Most of the propositions and questions to be found in philosophical works are not false but non-sensical.

William Wordsworth

⊢ 1770—1850 *English poet*

Why should not grave Philosophy be styled.
Herself, a dreamer of a kindred stock,
A dreamer, yet more spiritless and dull?
—[296]: Excursion (bk. III)

The bosom-weight, your stubborn gift,
That no philosophy can lift.
—[296]: Presentiments

23

Robert Zend

⊢ 1929—1985 *American philosopher*

Being a philosopher, I have a problem for every solution. —[297]

Bibliography

[1] Adams, H.B. (1918). *The Education of Henry Adams.* Oxford: Oxford University Press, reprint edition, 1999.

[2] Adams, D. (1996). *The Ultimate Hitchhiker's Guide.* Random House Value Publications.

[3] Letter, May 12, 1780, to his wife Abigail Adams, *The Book of Abigail and John: Selected Letters of the Adams Family, 1762-1784*, Northeastern University Press, 2002.

[4] Asimov, I. (1978).'My Own View' in *Asimov on Science Fiction*, ed. by R. Holdstock. Doubleday.

[5] Ayer, A.J. (1999). *Language, Truth and Logic.* Dover Publications; reprint edition, 1999.

[6] Aytoun, W.E. (1985). *Alchemist of the Golden Dawn: The Letters of the Revd W.A. Ayton to F.L. Gardner and Others, 1886-1905.* Aquarian Press.

[7] Bacon, F. (1998). *The Great Instauration and the Novum Organum.* Kessinger Publishing Company, 1998.

[8] Bacon, F. (1986). *The Essays.* Viking Press, reprint edition, 1986.

[9] Bacon, R. (1998). *The Opus Majus of Roger Bacon.* Trans. by Robert Belle Burke. Kessinger Publishing Company, reprint edition, 1998.

[10] Bais, A. (1991). *Niels Bohr's Times.* Oxford: Oxford University Press.

[11] Bambrough, R. (1984). 'The Scope of Reason: An Epistle to the Persians', *Objectivity and Cultural Divergence*, edited by S.C. Brown. Cambridge: Cambridge University Press.

[12] Bataille, G. (1985). *Visions of Excess: Selected Writings, 1927-1939*. University of Minnesota Press.

[13] Bentham, J. (1999). *'Legislator of the World': Writings on Codification, Law, and Education (The Collected Works of Jeremy Bentham)*. Oxford University Press.

[14] Berdyaev, N. (~1976). *Dream and Reality*. Publisher unknown.

[15] Berger, J. in 'The Soul and the Operator,' *Expressen* (Stockholm), March 19, 1990.

[16] Berkeley, G. (1988). *Principles of Human Knowledge / Three Dialogues*. New York: Penguin Books.

[17] Berlin, I. (1981). *Concepts and Categories: Philosophical Essays*. Curtis Brown Group Ltd.

[18] Bierce, A. (1998). *The Devil's Dictionary*. Oxford: Oxford University Press, reprint edition, 1998.

[19] Blackwell, A.B. (1875). *The Sexes Throughout Nature*. Hyperion Press, reprint edition, 1976.

[20] Blessington, M. (1971). 'The Confessions of an Elderly Lady,' *The Works of Lady Blessington*. AMS Press, reprint edition, 1971.

[21] Block, N. (1990). 'Troubles with Functionalism', *Mind and Cognition: A Reader*. Edited by W. Lycan. Blackwell Publishers.

[22] Bono, E.d. (1994). *De Bono's Thinking Course*. Facts on File. Revised edition.

[23] Boone, L. (1999). *Quotable Business: Over 2,800 Funny, Irreverent, and Insightful Quotations About Corporate Life*. Random House.

[24] Born, M. (1951). 'Natural Philosophy of Cause and Chance,' *The Restless Universe*. Dover Publications.

[25] Born, M. (1978). *My Life: Recollections of a Nobel Laureate*. Taylor & Francis.

[26] Boswell, J. (1993). *The Life of Samuel Johnson*. Alfred F. Knopf.

[27] Boyd, T.A. (2002). *Charles F. Kettering: A Biography*. Beard Books.

[28] Bradley, F.H. (1969). *Appearance and Reality*. Oxford: Oxford University Press, 2nd edition, 1969.

[29] *Chicago Tribune / New York Times Syndicate* quoted by Larry Wolters.

[30] Bruno, G. (1968). *De l'infinito, universo e mondi*. Trans. by D. Singer, *Giornardo Bruno, His Life and Thought etc.* New York.

[31] Butler, S. (2004). *Hudibras*. Free Books to Read.

[32] Campbell, T. (1972). *Poetical Works*. Ayer Company Publishers.

[33] Camus, A. (1991). *The Myth of Sisyphus and Other Essays*. Vintage Books, reissue edition, 1991.

[34] Canetti, E. (1973). *The Secret Heart of the Clock*. Farrar Straus & Giroux, reprint edition 1989.

[35] Carlyle, T. (1914). *Characteristics*. P.F. Collier & Son Company, 1909-14, reprint edition, New York: Barteleby.com, 2002.

[36] Carlyle, T. (2004). *Critical and Miscellaneous Essays: The Works of Thomas Carlyle — On History*. Kessinger Publishing Company.

[37] Carnap, R. (1995). *The University of Science*. Trans. by M. Black. Thoemmes Press, reprint edition, 1995.

[38] Carson, R. (1962). *The Silent Spring*. Mariner Books, reprint edition, 1994.

[39] Chamfort, S. (1980). *Maximes Et Pensees Caracteres Et Anecdot*. Gallimard French, reprint edition, 1980.

[40] Chase, A. (1966). *Perspectives*. Todd & Honeywell, reprint edition, 1966.

[41] Chesterton, G.K. (1907). 'Book of Job,' *The Collected Works of G.K. Chesterton, Volume 2: The Everlasting Man, St. Francis of Assisi, St. Thomas Aquinas*. Ignatius Press, reprint edition, 1907.

[42] Chesterton, C.K. (2001). *The Ballad of the White Horse*. House of Stratus Inc., reprint edition, 2001.

[43] Cicero, M.T. (1970). *Cicero: De Senectute, De Amicitia, De Divinatione*. Harvard University Press, reprint edition, 1970.

[44] Cicero, M.T. (1985). *The Nature of the Gods*. Viking Press, reissue edition, 1985.

[45] Cicero, M.T. (1998). *Scripta Quae Manserunt Omnia: Tusculanae Disputationes*. K.G. Saur, reprint edition, 1998.

[46] *Time*, February 15, 1971.

[47] Cole, W. (1999). *Random House Treasury of Humorous Quotations*. Random House Reference.

[48] Conway, A. (1996). *Principles of the Most Ancient and Modern Philosophy*. Cambridge University Press, reprint edition, 1996.

[49] Cooley, M. (1987). *City Aphorisms*, Fourth Selection. New York.

[50] *Washington Post*, August 2, 2001.

[51] Crane, S. (2004). 'Men, Women, and Boats,' underthe-sun.cc.

[52] Cronenberg, D. (1992). *Cronenberg on Cronenberg*. Faber & Faber, revised edition, 1997.

[53] Dennett, D.C. (1992). *The Intentional Stance*. MIT Press.

[54] Dennett, D.C. and Hofstadter, D. (1982). *The Minds Eye*. Penguin Books.

[55] Dennett, D.C. (1998). 'Out of the Armchair and Into the Field,' *Poetics Today*, vol. 9: 205-222.

[56] Descartes, R. (1996). *Discourse on the Method and Meditations on First Philosophy: And, Meditations on First Philosophy*. Yale University Press, reprint edition, 1996.

[57] Desmond, A. (1997). *Huxley: From Devil's Disciple to Evolution's High Priest*. Perseus Press.

[58] Dewey, J. (1986). *The Collected Works of John Dewey: Early, Middle, Later, Works, 1882-1953*. Edited by A.N. Shape. © by the Board of Trustess, Southern Illinois University Press.

[59] Diderot, D. (1997). Lettre á Falconet, *Letters to Sophie Volland*. Oxford University Press, reprint edition, 1997.

[60] Diderot, D. (1996). 'Observations on Drawing up of Laws,' *Selected Writings*, ed. by Lester G. Crocker, reprint edtion, 1966.

[61] Diogenes (1938). *Diogenes Laertius: Lives of Eminent Philosophers* (Loeb Classical Library #184). Harvard University Press.

[62] Le Douef, M. (1980). 'Women and Philosophy,' *French Feminist Thought*, ed. by T. Moi. Blackwell Publishers.

[63] Lord Dunsany (2004). *The Book of Wonder*. Bookshare.org.

[64] Durant, A. (1992) in *The Last Word—A Treasury of Women's Quotes*, ed. by C. Warner. Prentice Hall Trade.

[65] Durant, W. (1991). *Story of Philosophy: The Lives and Opinions of the World's Greatest Philosophers*. Pocket Books, reissue edition, 1991.

[66] Edwards, P. (1989). 'Heidegger's Quest for Being,' *Philosophy* (1989).

[67] Einstein, A. (2000). *The Expanded Quotable Einstein.* Edited by A. Calaprice. Princeton University Press

[68] Eliade, M. (1979). *The Forge and the Crucible: The Origins and Structures of Alchemy.* University of Chicago Press, 2nd edition, 1979.

[69] Eliot, G. (1994). *Middlemarch.* Penguin USA, reprint edition, 1994.

[70] Eliot, G. (1996). *Daniel Deronda.* Penguin USA, reprint edition, 1996.

[71] Eliot, T. S. (1976). *Knowledge and Experience in the Philosophy of F.H. Bradley.* Columbia University Press.

[72] Elliot, H. (1998). *Modern Science and Materialism,* Voices of Wisdom, ed. G. Kessler. Wadsworth Publishing Company.

[73] *Journal,* July 10, 1841.

[74] Emerson, R.W. (1996). 'Plato; or, the Philosopher,' *Representative Men.* Belknap Press, reprint edition, 1996.

[75] Emerson, R.W. (2001). *Journals of Ralph Waldo Emerson, 1845-1848.* Replica Books.

[76] Emerson, R.W. (1860). 'Wealth,' *The Conduct of Life.* Reprint Services Corp.

[77] Emerson, R.W. (1996). *Emerson: The Mind on Fire,* Robert D. Richardson, University of California Press, reprint edition, 1996.

[78] Epictetus (1994). *Discourses of Epictetus.* Trans. by G. Long. West Richard, reprint edition, 1994.

[79] Feuerabend, P. (1975). *Against Method.* Verso Books, 3rd edition, 1993.

[80] Feynman, R.P. (1967). *The Character of Physical Law.* Cambridge: MIT Press.

[81] Feynman, R.P. (1953). *Six Easy Pieces—Essentials of Physics Explained by Its Most Brilliant Teacher.* Introduction by P. Davies. Helix Books.

[82] Feynman, R.P. (1999). *The Pleasure of Finding Things Out.* Helix Books.

[83] Flew, A. (1917). *Atheistic Humanism.* Amherst, NY: Prometheus Books, reprint edition, published in1993.

[84] Flew, A. (2001). *Merely Mortal?: Can You Survive Your Own Death?* Promethean Press, reprint edition, 2001.

[85] Fodor, J. (1985). 'Banish disContent,' *Mind and Cognition*, edited by J. Butterfield. Cambridge University Press, 1985.

[86] Letter to David Hartley, December 4, 1789, *The Ingenious Dr. Franklin: Selected Scientific Letters of Benjamin Franklin*, edited by Nathan G. Goodman. University of Pennsylvania Press, 2000.

[87] Dialogue Between Franklin and the Gout, October 22, 1780, *The Ingenious Dr. Franklin: Selected Scientific Letters of Benjamin Franklin*, edited by Nathan G. Goodman. University of Pennsylvania Press, 2000.

[88] Quoted in *Scientific American.*

[89] Frei, C. (2001). *Hans J. Morgenthau—An Intellectual Biography.* Louisiana State University Press.

[90] Galbraith, J.K. (1994). *A Short History of Financial Euphoria.* Penguin USA, reprint edition, 1994.

[91] Galilei, G. 'Opere Il Saggiatore,' *The Controversy of the Comets of 1618. Galileo Galilei, Horatio Grassi, Mario Guiducci, Johann Kepler*, ed. and trans. by Drake, Stillman, & C. D. O'Malley. Philadelphia: University of Pensylvania Press, 1960.

[92] Letter to Cristina di Lorena, *Letters to Father: Suor Maria Celeste to Galileo, 1623-1633.* Walker & Co., 2001.

[93] *Saturday Evening Post*, December 1, 1962.

[94] Gaugain, P. (1949). *Intimate Journals*, transl. by Van Wyck Brooks, 1923. Liveright Publishing Corp, reprint edition, 1949.

[95] Gassett, J.O.Y. (1996). 'In Search of Goethe from Within', *Worlds of Existentialism: A Critical Reader*. Edited by M. Friedman. Humanity Books.

[96] Gaylor, A.L. (ed.) (1997). 'A Few Reasons for Renouncing Christianity and Professing and Disseminating Infidel Opinions,' by Emma Martin, excerpted from *Women Without Superstition*: *No Gods—No Masters*. Freedom From Religion Foundation, Inc., 2nd edition, 1997.

[97] Gellner, E. (1980). *Words and things: an examination of, and an attack on, linguistic philosophy*. Routledge & Kegan Paul, revised edition, 1980.

[98] Gilson, E. (1955). *History of Christian Philosophy in the Middle Ages*. Random House.

[99] Gladstone, W.E. (1993). *The Gladstone Diaries: 1825-1832: 1833-1839*. Oxford: Oxford University Press.

[100] Glymour, C. (1992). *Thinking Things Through*. Cambridge: MIT Press.

[101] Goethe, J. W. v. (1994). *Faust, Goethe: The Collected Works*, Vol 2. Princeton University Press, 1994.

[102] Goldsmith, O. (1979). *Good Natured Man and She Stoops to Conquer*. Arden Library.

[103] Goodman, N. (1977). *The Structure of Appearance*. Kluwer Academic Publishers. Reprinted with kind permission of Kluwer Academic Publishers.

[104] Goldstein, R. (1983). *The Mind-Body Problem*. Random House.

[105] Hacking, I. (1983). *Representing and Intervening*. Cambridge: Cambridge University Press.

[106] Hamilton, W. (1952). *Discussions on Philosophy*. Oxford: Oxford University Press.

[107] Hamlyn, D. W. (1989). *History of Western Philosophy.* Penguin Books.

[108] Hampton, C. (1989). *Dangerous Liaisons.* Faber & Faber.

[109] Haught, J.A. (ed.) (1996). 'Rufus K. Noyes, Views of Religion,' in *2000 Years of Disbelief: Famous People With the Courage to Doubt.* Amherst, NY: Prometheus Books, published in 1996.

[110] Hawking, S. (1988). *A Brief History of Time.* Bantam Books. Used by permission of The Random House Group Limited.

[111] Hazlitt, W. (1999). *Selected Writings.* Oxford: Oxford University Press.

[112] Hegel, G.W.F. (1998). *The Science of Logic.* Trans. by A.V. Miller. Humanity Books.

[113] Heidegger, M. (1992). *The Metaphysical Foundations of Logic.* Trans. by. M. Heim. Indiana University Press, Bloomington & Indianapolis, reprint edition, 1992.

[114] Hein, P. (1968). *The Ultimate Wisdom, Grooks II.* Doubleday.

[115] Heisenberg, W. (1958). *Physics and Philosophy.* Amherst, NY: Prometheus Books, reprint edition, published in 1999.

[116] Heschel, A. J. (1965). *Who is Man?* Stanford University Press. Copyright © 1965, Abraham Joshua Heschel

[117] Hintikka, J. (2003). 'Epistemology without Knowledge and Belief,' *draft*: 35 pp.

[118] Hobbes, T. (1993). *Collected Works of Thomas Hobbes.* Edited by W. Molesworth. Routledge.

[119] Hodges, W. (1998). 'An Editor Recalls Some Hopeless Papers,' *The Bulletin on Symbolic Logic*, Vol. 4, No. 1, March 1998.

[120] *Today*, BBC Radio 4.

[121] Holmes Jr., O. W. *Techniques of Persuasion: From Propaganda to Brainwashing*. Viking Press.

[122] Hook, S. (1994). *From Hegel to Marx: Studies in the Intellectual Development of Karl Marx*. Columbia University Press.

[123] Hubbard. E. (1999). *Elbert Hubbard's Scrap Book: Containing the Inspired and Inspiring Selections Gathered During a Life Time of Discriminating Reading for His Own Use*. Firebird Press.

[124] Hume, D. (1983). *Letters of David Hume*. Garland Publishers, 1983.

[125] Hume, D. (1987). *Essays, Moral, Political, and Literary*. Liberty Fund, Inc. revised edition, 1987.

[126] Hume, D. (1989). *An Inquiry Concerning Human Understanding*. Edited by P.H. Nidditich. New York: Oxford University Press.

[127] Hume, D. (1990). *Treatise on Human Nature*. AMS Press, reprint edition, 1990.

[128] Hume, D. (1998). *Principal Writings on Religion Including Dialogues Concerning Natural Religion and the Natural History of Religion*. Oxford University Press, 192nd edition.

[129] Huxley, A. (2004). *A Brave New World*. Read Print.

[130] Inge, W.R. (1980). *Outspoken Essays, Second Series*. Ayer Company Publishers.

[131] Jacobi, K.G. (1988). *Mathematical Maxims and Minims*, ed. by N. Rose. Raleigh NC: Rome Press Inc.

[132] James, W. (1897). 'The Will To Believe', *William James: Writings 1878-1899 : Psychology, Briefer Course / The Will to Believe / Talks to Teachers and Students / Essays*. Library of America.

[133] James, W. (1907). 'Pragmatism', in *William James: Writings 1902-1910 : The Varieties of Religious Experience / Pragmatism / A Pluralistic Universe / The Meaning of Truth / Some Problems of Philosophy / Essays*. Library of America, reprint edition, 1988.

[134] James, W. (1975). *The Collected Works of William James: Essays in Radical Empiricism*. Harvard University Press.

[135] James, W. (1982). *The Collected Works of William James: Essays in Religion and Morality*. Harvard University Press.

[136] James, W. (1992). *The Letters of William James* (Notable American Authors Series). Reprint Services Corp.

[137] Jung, C.C. and Pauli, W. (1955). *The Interpretation of Nature and the Psyche*, London.

[138] Kallen, H.M. (1980). *William James and Henri Bergson: A Study in Contrasting Theories of Life*. AMS Press, reprint edition, 1980.

[139] Kant, I. (2004). *The Critique of Pure Reason*. Infomotions.com. Translated by J.M.D. Meikleton.

[140] Keats, J. (1990). *Lamia 1820*. Woodstock Books.

[141] Kepler, J. (1609). *Astronomia Nova*. Cambridge University Press, reprint edition, 1992.

[142] Keyes, D. (1999). *Chameleon Christianity: Moving Beyond Safety and Conformity*. Baker Book House.

[143] Kierkegaard, S.A. (1978). *The Journals of Søren Kirkegaard*. Edited by Howard & Edna Hong. Indiana University Press, Bloomington and Indianapolis.

[144] Kierkegaard, S.A. (1983). *The Concept of Irony*. Octagon Books.

[145] Kierkegaard, S.A. (1992). *Either/Or*. Penguin USA, reprint edition, 1992.

[146] Kierkegaard, S.A. (1996). *Papers and Journals: A Selection.* Trans. by A. Hannay. Penguin USA, reprint edition, 1996.

[147] Krutch, J.W. (2000). *Herbal.* David R. Godine Publishers.

[148] Lakoff. G. (1999). *Philosophy in the Flesh.* New York: Basic Books.

[149] Landor, W.S. (1886). 'Epicurus, Leontion, and Ternissa,' *Imaginary conversations and poems: a selection.* Walter Scott, 1886.

[150] Langer, S. (1942). *Philosophy in a New Key.* Harvard University Press, 3rd. edition, 1957.

[151] Levinas, E. (1984). Levinas in *Dialogues with Contemporary Continental Thinkers,* ed. by Richard Kearney. Manchester University Press.

[152] Levinas, E. (1998). *Otherwise than Being or Beyond Essence.* Duquesne University Press.

[153] Lewes, G.H. (1979). *The Biographical History of Philosophy.* Arden Library.

[154] Lewis, C.S. (1994). 'Allegory of Love,' *The Chronicles of Narnia.* Oxford University Press.

[155] Timothy Leary in *The London Evening Standard,* 1989.

[156] Henri Lebesgue in *Scientific American,* 211, September, 1964.

[157] Lichtenberg, G. (1983). *The Reflections of Lichtenberg,* trans. N. Allison. Lawrence Erlbaum.

[158] Lipmann, W. (1962). *A Preface to Politics.* University of Michigan Press.

[159] *Edinburgh Review,* August, 1825.

[160] Mackey, A. (1994). *A Dictionary of Scientific Quotations.* London: Institute of Physics Publishing.

[161] Mackie, J.L. (1977). *Ethics: Inventing Right and Wrong.* New York: Penguin.

[162] Maistre, J. d. (1821). *Les Soirées de Saint-Pétersbourg*, Fifth Dialogue.

[163] *The Philosophers' Magazine*, Summer 1998.

[164] *The Philosophers' Magazine*, Spring 2000.

[165] Marx, K. (1843). 'For a Ruthless Criticism of Everything Existing,' *The Communist Manifesto*. Signet Classic, reprint edition, 1998.

[166] Marx, K. and Engels, F. (1845-6). *The German Ideology.* Amherst, NY: Prometheus Books, reprint edition, published in 1989.

[167] McCosh, J. (1875). *Scottish Philosophy, Bibliographical, Expository, Critical, from Hutcheson to Hamilton.* AMS Press, Incorporated.

[168] Medawar, P. B. (1983). *Aristotle to Zoos.* Cambridge, MA: Harvard University Press.

[169] Mencken, H. L. (1956). *Minority Report: H.L. Mencken's Notebooks.* Johns Hopkins University Press, reprint edition, 1977.

[170] *The Philosophers' Magazine*, Summer 1999.

[171] Milton, J. (2004). *Paradise Lost.* Online Literature Library.

[172] Montaigne, M. d. *1575 ESSAYS.* Translated by Charles Cotton. URL: http://oregonstate.edu/instruct/phl302/texts/montaigne/m-essays_contents.html.

[173] Muller, H. J. (1952). *The Uses of the Past: Profiles of Former Societies.* Oxford University Press.

[174] Murdoch, I. (1987). *The Book and the Brotherhood.* Penguin USA, reprint edition, 1989.

[175] Murdoch, I. (1986). *Acastos: Two Platonic Dialogues.* Viking Press, 1st American edition, 1986.

[176] Newman, J. H. (1978). *A curriculum evaluation of Black studies in relation to student knowledge of Afro-American history and culture.* R. and E. Research Associates.

[177] Newton, I. (1952). *Opticks: Or a Treatise of the Reflections Inflections and Colours of Light.* Dover Publications, reprint edition, 1952.

[178] Nietzsche, F. (1974). *The Gay Science: With a Prelude in Rhymes and an Appendix of Songs.* Trans. by W. Kaufman. Vintage Books, reprint edition, 1974.

[179] Nietzsche, F. (1978). *Thus Spoke Zarathustra.* Trans. by J. Hollingdale. Penguin USA, reprint edition, 1978.

[180] Nietzsche, F. (1989). *Beyond Good and Evil.* Trans. by W. Kaufman. Vintage Books, reprint edition, 1989.

[181] Nietzsche, F. (1990). *Twilight of the Idols and the Anti Christ.* Trans. by J. Hollingdale. Viking Press, reissue edition, 1990.

[182] Nietzsche, F. (1996). *Ecce Homo: How One Becomes What One Is.* Trans. by J. Hollingdale. Penguin USA, reprint edition, 1996.

[183] Nietzsche, F. (1996). *Human, All Too Human.* Trans. by J. Hollingdale. Penguin USA, reprint edition, 1996.

[184] Nietzsche, F. (1996). *Philosophy in the Tragic Age of the Greeks.* Trans. by M. Cowan. Regnery Publishing, Inc., reprint edition, 1996.

[185] Novalis (1997). *Novalis: Philosophical Writings.* Trans. by M. Mahony Stoljar. State University of New York Press.

[186] Nozick, R. (1981). *Philosophical Explanations.* Harvard University Press.

[187] Oakeshott, M. (1986). *Experience and its Modes.* Cambridge University Press, reprint edition, 1986.

[188] Oppenheimer, J.R. (1958). 'The Tree of Knowledge,' *Harper's*, 1958.

[189] Origen (~1950). *De Principiis*. By Nicola Pace. La Nuova Italia, 1a edition.

[190] Ouspensky, P.D. (1997). *A New Model of the Universe: Principles of the Psychological Method in Its Application to Problems of Science, Religion, and Art.* Dover Publications.

[191] *The Philosophers' Magazine*, Autumn 2000.

[192] Paracelsus, P.A. (1584). *Buch von der Gebärung.* Reprinted in *Paracelsus*, edited by J. Jacobi and trans. by N. Guterman. Princeton University Presss, reprint edition, 1995.

[193] Parkinson, C.N. (1996). *Parkinson's Law.* Buccaneer Books.

[194] Pascal, B. (1978). *The Thoughts of Blaise Pascal.* Greenwood Publishing Group, reprint edition, 1978.

[195] Pasternak, B. (1957). *Doctor Zhivago.* Pantheon Books, reprint edition, 1997.

[196] Peirce, C.S. (1999). *Collected Papers of Charles Sanders Peirce.* Edited by P. Weiss. Thoemmes Printers.

[197] Peirce, C.S. (1958). 'The Fixation of Belief,' *Charles S. Peirce: Selected Writings.* Edited by P. Wiener. New York: Dover Publications.

[198] Quoted from *Wisdom of the Ages at Your Fingertips*, MCR software, 1995.

[199] Pirsig, R. (1984). *Zen and the Art of Motorcycle Maintenance: An Inquiry into Values.* Bantam Books, reissue edition, 1984. Used by permission of The Random House Group Limited.

[200] Planck, M. (1998). *Eight Lectures on Theoretical Physics.* Trans. by A.P. Wills. Dover Publications.

[201] Plato (1980). *The Works of Plato.* Edited by T. Taylor. Garland Publishers.

[202] Plotinus (1991). *The Enneads.* Penguin USA, reprint, abridged edition, 1991.

[203] Plutarch (1993). *Essays.* Penguin USA.

[204] Poincare, H. (2001). *Science and Method.* St. Augustine's Press, reprint edition, 2001.

[205] Polanyi, M. (1963). *The Study of Man.* University of Chicago Press, 1963.

[206] Popper, K. (1971). *The Open Society and Its Enemies.* Princeton University Press, 5th rev. edition, 1971.

[207] Pratchett, T. (1994). *Small Gods.* Harper Mass Market Paperbacks, reprint edition, 1994.

[208] Prokosch, F. (1983). 'Style,' *Voices: A Memoir.* Noonday Press.

[209] Putnam, H. (1985). *Realism and Reason.* Cambridge University Press, reprint edition, 1985.

[210] *The Philosophers' Magazine,* Summer, 2001.

[211] Letter to Princess Victoria of Hesse, August 22, 1883.

[212] Quine, W. (1964). *Word and Object.* MIT Press.

[213] Quine, W. (1977). *Ontological Relativity and Other Essays.* Columbia University Press.

[214] Quine, W. (1986). *Theories and Things.* Belknap Press.

[215] Quine, W. (1989). *Methods of Logic.* Harvard University Press, fourth edition, 1989.

[216] Quinton, A. (1882). *Thoughts and Thinkers.* Holmes & Meier Publishers, Inc.

[217] Ramsey, F. (1978). *Foundations: Essays in Philosophy, Logic, Mathematics, and Economics.* Amherst, NY: Prometheus Books, published in1978.

[218] Rauch, J. (1995). *Kindly Inquisitors: The New Attacks on Free Thought*. University of Chicago Press, reprint edition, 1995.

[219] Raudsepp, E. (1984). *The World's Best Thoughts on Success & Failure*. Price Stern Sloan Publishers.

[220] Reade, W. (1872). *The Martyrdom of Man*. De Young Press, reprint edition, 1997.

[221] Reid, T. (2001). *Thomas Reid: An Inquiry into the Human Mind on the Principles of Common Sense*. Pennsylvania State University Press, critical edition, 2001.

[222] Rescher, N. (1985). *The Strife of Systems: An Essay on the Grounds and Implications of Philosophical Diversity*. University of Pittsburgh Press.

[223] Rochefoucauld, F.D. (1982). *Maxims*. Viking Press, reprint edition, 1982.

[224] Robertson, J. (ed.) (2005). *Philosophical Works of Francis Bacon*. Ayer Company Publishers.

[225] Rorty, R. (1985). *Consequences of Pragmatism: Essays, 1972-1980*. University of Minnesota Press.

[226] Rorty, R. (1998). *Truth and Progress: Philosophical Papers*. Cambridge University Press.

[227] *The Philosophers' Magazine*, Autumn 1999.

[228] Rousseau, J.-R. (2004). *The Social Contract or Principles of Political Right*. Constitution Society

[229] Russell, B. (1950). *Unpopular Essays*. Routledge.

[230] Bertrand Russell in the *Observer*, Sayings of the Week, April 24, 1955.

[231] Russell, B. (1956). 'The Philosophy of Logical Atomism,' *Logic and Knowledge: Essays, 1901-1950*, ed. R.C. Marsh. London: Allen & Unwin, reprinted by Routledge, 1st edition, 1988.

[232] Bertrand Russell in the *Observer*, Sayings of the Year 1962.

[233] Russell, B. (1988). *Essays*. Routledge, 1st edition.

[234] Russell, B. (1992). *Theory of Knowledge*. Routledge, 1st edition.

[235] Russell, B. (1998). *The Problems of Philosophy*. Oxford: Oxford University Press, 2nd edition.

[236] Ryle, G. (1954). *Dilemmas*. Cambridge University Press.

[237] Ryle, G. (1984). *The Concept of Mind*. University of Chicago Press, reprint edition, 1984.

[238] Sade, M.de. (1988). *Juliette*. Grove/Atlantic Inc., 1988. Originally published as *L'Histoire de Juliette, ou les Prosprits du Vice* in 1797.

[239] Sade, M.de. (1999). *The Misfortunes of Virtue*. Oxford: Oxford University Press. Originally published in 1787.

[240] Santayana, G. (1955). *Skepticism and Animal Faith: Introduction to a System of Philosophy*. Dover Publications.

[241] Saxton, M. (1995). *Louisa May Alcott: A Modern Biography*. Noonday Press.

[242] Schlegel, F. (1971). *Friedrich Schlegel's Lucinde and the Fragments*. University of Minnesota Press.

[243] Schmidt, M. (2000). *Lives of the Poets*. Random House.

[244] Selden, J. (1955). *Table-Talk*. Ayer Company Publishers.

[245] Shakespeare, W. (2004). *The Complete Works of William Shakespeare*. Classic Literature Library.

[246] Shaw, G.B. (1975). *Collected Plays With Their Prefaces: Definitive Edition in Seven Volumes*. Dodd Mead.

[247] Shaw, G.B. (2001). *Man and Superman: A Comedy and a Philosophy*. Penguin USA, reprint edition, 2001.

[248] Smart, J.J.C. (1989). 'Philosophy and Scientific Realism,' *Our Place in the Universe: A Metaphysical Discussion.* Blackwell Publishers.

[249] Smith, A. (1999). *The Theory of Moral Sentiments Or, an Essay/2 Volumes Bound in 1 Book: Towards an Analysis of the Principles, by Which Men Naturally Judge Concerning.* Regnery Publications.

[250] Smith, G.H. (2000). *Why Atheism?* Amherst, NY: Prometheus Books, published in 2000.

[251] Spencer, H. (1982). *The Man Versus the State: With Six Essays on Government, Society, and Freedom.* Liberty Fund, Inc.

[252] Spengler, O. (1991). *The Decline of the West.* Oxford University Press.

[253] Stefansson, V. (2001). *Writing on Ice: The Ethnographic Notebooks of Vilhjalmur Stefansson.* University Press of New England.

[254] Stenger, J.V. (1990). *Physics and Psychics: The Search for a World Beyond the Senses.* Amherst, NY: Prometheus Books, published in 1990.

[255] Stephens, J. (1998). *The Crock of Gold.* Dover Publications.

[256] Stevens, W. (1990). 'Adagia,' *Opus Posthumous.* Vintage Books, revised edition, 1990.

[257] 'The Figure of the Youth as Virile Poet', speech, August, 1943.

[258] Stoppard, T. (1969). *Albert's Bridge.* Faber & Faber, reprint edition, 1997.

[259] Stoppard, T. (1986). *Jumpers.* Grove/Atlantic, Inc., reprint edition, 1989.

[260] *Readers' Digest,* May 1995,

[261] Strawson, P.F. (1987). *Skepticism and Naturalism: Some Varieties.* Columbia University Press, reprint edition, 1987.

[262] *Prospect*, August/September, 2001.

[263] *The Philosophers' Magazine*, Autumn 2000.

[264] Tennyson, A.L. (1998). *The Works of Alfred Lord Tennyson.* NTC/Contemporary Publishing, reissue edition, 1998.

[265] Thomson, J. (1971). *The Poetical Works of James Thomson.* Scholarly Press.

[266] Thoreau, H.D. (2001). *Walden and Other Writings.* Metro Books.

[267] Thorpe, W.H. (1983). *Beyond Reductionism.* Irvington Publications.

[268] Thurber, J. (1989). 'Thinking Ourselves Into Trouble,' pt. 1, *Collecting Himself: James Thurber on Writing and Writers, Humor, and Himself.* HarperCollins.

[269] Tolstoi, L.V. (1985). *The Kingdom of God Is Within You.* University of Nebraska Press.

[270] Twain, M. (2004). *The $30,000 Bequest.* Classic Literature Library.

[271] Quoted in Natalie Angier, 'Confessions of a Lonely Atheist,' *New York Times Magazine*, January 14, 2001.

[272] Vizinczey, S. (1974). 'Good Faith and Bad,' *Sunday Telegraph*, London, April, 21, 1974; reprinted in *Truth and Lies in Literature.* H. Hamilton.

[273] Voltaire, F.-M. A. (1990). *The best known works of Voltaire; the complete romances, including Candide, The philosophy of history, The ignorant philosopher, Dialogues and Philosophic criticisms.* Unknown Binding.

[274] Waismann, F. (1979). *Ludwig Wittgenstein and the Vienna Circle: Conversations Recorded by Friedrich Waismann*, edited by Brian McGuinness. Barnes & Noble, 1979.

[275] *The Philosophers' Magazine*, Summer 1999.

[276] *The Guardian*, January 26, 2000.

[277] Warwick, K. (2002). *I, Cyborg*. Century.

[278] Watts, A.J. (1983). *The Way of Liberation*. Weatherhill.

[279] Weil, S. (1943). *First and Last Notebooks*. Oxford: Oxford University Press.

[280] Weil, S. (1985). *The Simone Weil Reader*. Moyer Bell Ltd.

[281] Weinberg, S. (1992). *Dreams of a Final Theory. The Scientist's Search for the Ultimate Laws of Nature*. New York: Vintage Books.

[282] Weller, T. (1987). *Culture Made Stupid*. Houghton Mifflin Company.

[283] Whitehead, A. N. (1985). *Process and Reality*. Free Press, corrected edition, 1985.

[284] Whitehead, A. N. (1938). *Modes of Thought*. Free Press, reissue edition, 1985.

[285] Whitehead, A. N. (1994). *The Concept of Nature*. Cambridge University Press, reissue edition, 1994.

[286] Wiener, N. (1986). *Norbert Wiener: Collected Works— Vol. 4: Cybernetics, Science, and Society; Ethics, Aesthetics, and Literary Criticism; Book Reviews and Obituaries*. MIT Press.

[287] Wigner, E.P. (1960). 'The Unreasonable Effectiveness of Mathematics in the Natural Sciences,' *Communications in Pure and Applied Mathematics*, Vol. 13, No. 1 (February, 1960).

[288] Wigner, E.P. (1998). *The Collected Works of Eugene Paul Wigner: Historical, Philosophical, and Socio-Political Papers: Socio-Political Reflections and Civil Defense.* Springer Verlag.

[289] Wilde, O. (1891). *The Artist As Critic: Critical Writings of Oscar Wilde.* University of Chicago Press, reprint edition, 1983.

[290] Wilder, T. (1942). *The Skin of Our Teeth.* Harper Perennial, reprint edition, 1998.

[291] Wittgenstein, L. (1958). *The Brown and the Blue Book.* Basil Blackwell.

[292] Wittgenstein, L. (1984). *Culture and Value.* University of Chicago Press, reprint edition, 1984.

[293] Wittgenstein, L. (1984). *Philosophical Investigations.* Prentice Hall, 3rd edition, 1999.

[294] Wittgenstein, L. (2001). *Tractatus Logico-Philosophicus.* Routledge, 2nd edition, 2001.

[295] *The Philosophers' Magazine,* Autumn 1999.

[296] Wordworth, W. (2004). *Complete Poetical Works.* everypoet.com.

[297] Zend, R. (1990). *Daymares: Selected Fictions on Dreams and Time.* Ronsdale Printers.

Acknowledgments

- Prof. Jaakko Hintikka
- Prof. Melvin Fitting
- Prof. Raymond M. Smullyan
- Prof. Kevin Warwick
- Prof. Lou Marinoff
- Dr. Douglas B. Quine (Literary Executor, W.v. Quine Estate, http://www.wvquine.org)
- Prof. Catherine Z. Elgin, Graduate School of Education, Harvard University (holder of literary rights to the works of Nelson Goodman)
- The Society of Authors, on behalf of the Bernard Shaw Estate
- Hackett Publishing Company
- Georges Borchardt, Inc., Literary Agency
- Oxford University Press
- Macmillan UK
- Random House, Inc.
- The Random House Group Limited
- Beard Books
- Rosemary A. Thurber

- The Barbara Hogenson Agency, Inc.
- Northeastern University Press
- Association for Symbolic Logic
- A.P. Watt Literary Agents
- The Royal Literary Fund
- Emma Martin
- Massachusetts Historical Society
- United Artists
- Curtis Brown Group Ltd.
- Regnery Publishing, Inc.
- Wh. Smith Publishers
- Read Print, http://www.readprint.com
- Dover Publications
- Greenwood Publishing Group
- Aquarian Press
- Kessinger Publishing Company
- Viking Press
- Cambridge University Press
- University of Minnesota Press
- Infomotions.com, http://infomotions.com
- Expressen
- Penguin Books Ltd.
- Penguin Putnam Inc.
- Hyperion Press
- AMS Press, Inc.

- Blackwell Publishing Ltd.
- Taylor & Francis
- Constitution Society, http://www.constitution.org/
- Knopf Publishing Group
- Chicago Tribune / New York Times Syndicate
- Ayer Company Publishers
- Classic Literature Library, http://www.classic-literature.co.uk/
- Farrar Straus & Giroux
- Thoemmes Press
- P.F. Collier and Son Company
- Benetech Bookshare.org, http://www.bookshare.org
- Bartleby.com
- Mariner Books
- Gallimard French
- Bodley Head
- Todd & Honeywell
- Ignatius Press
- everypoet.com, http://www.everypoet.com
- House of Stratus Inc.
- Harvard University Press
- K.G. Saur Verlag GmBh / A Part of the Thomson Corporation
- TIME Reprints and Permissions
- The Washington Post
- Faber & Faber
- Online Literature Library, http://www.literature.org/

- The MIT Press
- Poetics Today
- Underthesun, http://www.underthesun.cc/
- Free Books to Read, http://www.freebookstoread.com/
- Perseus Press
- Yale University Press
- Southern Illinois University Press
- Center for Dewey Studies
- Harper Perennial
- Prentice Hall
- Pocket Books
- Philosophy
- Princeton University Press
- The University of Chicago Press
- Facts on File
- Columbia University Press
- Wadsworth Publishing Company
- Journal
- The Belknap Press of Harvard University Press
- Replica Books
- Reprint Services Corp.
- University of Nebraska Press
- University of California Press
- West Richard
- Helix Books

- Verso Books
- Prometheus Books
- Promethean Press
- University of Pennsylvania Press
- Scientific American
- Louisiana State University Press
- Liveright Publishing Corp.
- Walker & Co.
- Saturday Evening Post
- Isaiah Berlin Literary Trust
- Humanity Books
- Freedom from Religion Foundation, Inc. / Annie Laurie Gaylor
- Routledge
- Kluwer Academic Publishers
- Bantam Books
- Indiana University Press, Bloomington & Indianapolis
- Stanford University Press
- Doubleday
- Firebird Press
- Garland Publishers
- Liberty Fund, Inc.
- Harper-Collins
- Rome Press Inc.
- Library of America
- Woodstock Books

- Baker Book House
- Octagon Books
- Outlet
- David R. Godine Publishers
- Basic Books, part of Perseus Books Group
- Walter Scott
- Manchester University Press
- Duquesne University Press
- Arden Library
- Lawrence Earlbaum
- University of Michigan Press
- The London Evening Standard
- Edinburgh Review
- Institute of Physics Publishing
- The Philosophers' Magazine
- Signet Classic
- Johns Hopkins University Press
- R. and E. Research Associates
- State University of New York Press
- Vintage Books
- Regnery Publishing Inc.
- Harper's
- Buccaneer Books
- Greenword Publishing Group
- St. Augustine's Press

- Pantheon Books
- MCR Software
- Harper Mass Market Paperbacks
- Noonday Press
- University of Chicago Press
- Holmes & Meir Publishers
- St. Martin's Press
- Price Stern Sloan Publishers
- De Young Press
- Pennsylvania State Univesity Press
- University of Pittsburgh Press
- Wiley
- The Observer
- BBC – British Broadcasting Company
- Grove/Atlantic, Inc.
- Augustus M. Kelley Publishers
- Addison-Wesley Publishing Company
- Dodd Mead
- University Press of New England
- Prospect
- NTC/Contemporary Publishing
- Scholarly Press
- Metro Books
- Irvington Publications
- New York Times Magazine

- Sunday Telegraph
- Barnes & Noble
- The Guardian
- Weatherwill
- Reader's Digest
- Moyer Bell Ltd.
- Houghton Mifflin Company
- Free Press
- Communications in Pure and Applied Mathematics
- Springer Verlag
- Rowman & Littlefield
- Ronsdale Printers

Index

Abstain, 41
absurd, 27
absurdity, 14
Academe, 14
Academy, 14
adversity, 125
after-world, 34
agriculture, 2
Albert the Great, 101
alien philosophies, 74
ambiguous, 118
America, 88
American empire, 88
American philosophy, 63
amusement, 99
aniseed trail, 131
answer, 135
ant, 8
Anthropic Principal, 121
anti-solipsist, 127
architecture, 2, 40
argument, 56
argument, counter-, 56
Aristotle, 56, 57, 80, 97, 101, 118, 136
armchair, 79
art, 51, 82
artillery, 114
aspirin, 46
Astrologers, 19
atheism, 7

Attribute, 44
Augustine, 116
Avicenna, 101

Babel, 4
bad brother Derrida, 116
balloon, 2
banality, 53
barmy, 131
baroque, 126
beast, 97
beauty, 51
bee, 8
Being, 37
believer, 126
Berkeley, 17
Bertrand Russell, 47, 135
boat, 111
bread, 4
brute curiosity, 114
bubble, 108
Buddha, 42
bumper sticker, 124
burden of proof, 4
burning, 9
business of philosophy, 8
butterfly, 3

cage, 19
cake, 3
cannibals, 32
Cantor, 62

carnivores, 139
Cartesian, 14
castle, 76
category-disciplines, 119
category-habits, 119
cats, 134
causation, 9
certainties, 95
cheerfulness, 37
children, 91
chimpanzees, 139
Chinese, 32
chinese, 3
Christians, 13
Cicero, 92
circle, 86
clear, 118
cleverness, 145
cobwebs, 8
'Cogito cogito ergo cogito sum', 14
'Cogito ergo sum', 14
commerce, 2
common sense, 10, 28, 29, 103, 112, 114, 146
commoner brains, 97
conclusion, 4
conduct, 47
confusion, 53
conjectures, 95
consciousness, 140
consistency, 40, 137
consolation, 30
cooking, 9
country, 47
criticism, 118
cure, 25
custom, 24
cutting a cake, 9
Cynics, 108

D. Philippus Feselius, 75
dark side (of philosophy), 88
death, 92, 130
definite, 118
Democritus, 115
demons, 31
Department of Mathematics, 5
Department of Philosophy, 5
depotism, 108
Descartes, 4, 14, 102, 116
destination, 119
destiny, 10
dialectic, 56, 100
Diogenes, 34
disappointment, 111
disciples, 119
discovery, 16
discretion, 125
discrimination, 82
dissapointing, 9
dissatisfaction, 111
divining rod, 3
dog, 11
dogs, 139
doubt, 104
dreamer, 147
dress suit, 4
drink, 73
drivel, 16
dull, 147
duplicate universe, 31
dust, 12

Earth, 129
ecstasies, 11
empathy, 139
empiricism, 4
empiricist, 122

Empress, 54
empty speculation, 101
English philosophy, 63
Epicureans, 108
epistemology, 25, 46, 61
equanimity, 144
erasers, 5
error, 5, 7
essence, 41
ethics, 24
Etienne Gilson, 109
etymologies, 37
Eudæmonidas, 106
Eureka, 5
evils, 115
exercise, 80
($\exists x$), 112
existence, 112, 145
experience, 24
experimental psychology, 129
expert, 15

fairies, 64
faith, 19
fallibilism, 127
falsehood, 131
fantasy, 31, 101
farmer, 134
Father Parmenides, 116
feasting, 92
feudalism, 80
fiction, 26
final theory, 141
finality, 130
fireworks, 54
flybottle, 146
fog, 87
fool, 31, 47
football, 14
footmarks, 119

footnotes, 143
four-dimensional geometry, 143
Fourier, 69
Frege, 116
French, 32
French philosophy, 63
freshness, 59
friendship, 82
'fuck', 4

gatekeeper, 10
genera, 8
geography, 2
Germans, 32
glasses, 146
glossogonous metaphysics, 38
gnostics, 13
God, 38, 47, 100, 102, 117
god, 97
good sense, 33
graffiti, 4
grammar, 95
grand book, 49
Greek philosophers, 142
gunpowder, 114

happiness, 41
hares, 11
Harvey, 44
hat, 3
heaven, 67, 125
Hegel, 99, 116, 124
Heidegger, 37, 52
hell, 67
Hermes, 19
highway, 58
historians, 15
history, 7, 109
hobgoblins, 64
Hölderlin, 37

holiday, 147
homesickness, 97
horse, 53
hounds of heaven, 131
humility, 91
humor, 16
hunter, 134
husband, 40
'hyphenitis', 38

'I', 50
'iatrogenic', 89
ideology, 44
ignorance, 5, 64, 91
illness, 145
illusion, 65
inconclusiveness, 126
incredulity, 34
individuating objects, 46
infallibilism, 127
infinity, 4, 36
information age, 80
innate, 13
inquiry, 5, 104, 114
insights, 11
insulting, 9
Introduction to Metaphysics, 37
introspection, 60
intuition pump, 31
iron, 146

jackasses, 90
jazz, 15
Johnson, 17
jokes, 5, 146
jollity, 92

Kant, 57, 96, 116
Kepler, 49
kings, 99

knowledge, 5, 52, 56, 57, 91

language, 49, 55, 131
laughter, 11
law of triviality, 102
laziness, 113
leather, 29
Legislation, 10
Liar paradox, 46
liars, 101
liberty, 47
life, 59, 67, 117
literature, 5
Lithic Principals, 122
logic, 7, 10, 14, 24, 25, 35, 51, 64, 77, 138
logic of confirmation, 46
logical, 130
Logical Analysis, 25
logical clarification, 146
logician, 114
Louis Armstrong, 15
love, 135
lunatic, 13

machines, 127
man, 64, 86
masturbation, 87
materialism, 144
mathematician, 81
mathematicians, 99
mathematics, 2, 3, 7, 49, 62, 69, 99, 128
medical man, 90
medical scientist, 89
medical treatment, 89
medicine, 25, 90
Medicos, 75
memory, 95
men of dogmas, 7
men of experiment, 7

Merleau-Ponty, 52
metaphysical fox, 131
metaphysician, 6
metaphysics, 2, 6, 9, 17, 24, 63, 64, 90, 105, 137
Middle Ages, 129
Midgley, 85
military, 62
mind, 24, 69, 73, 145
misfortunes, 144
mistress, 40
monism, 144
monsters, 8
moral philosophy, 49, 92
moralists, 56
mortals, 100
mothers, 131
mountain, 87
mountaineer, 87
mouth, 38
Mrs. Christine Ladd Franklin, 119
music, 2, 10, 40, 64
musician, 106
musket, 114
mystical vision, 11
myth, 44

nation, 74
natural history, 2
'natural number', 62
natural philosophy, 7, 101
Nature, 101
Nature's pilot, 126
naval architecture, 2
navigation, 2
Neurath, 111
Newton, 44
Nietzsche, 37
nonsense, 64

novelists, 56
nutshell, 57

objections, 86
obvious, 118
okapi, 12
old woman, 146
ontology, 42
opiate, 76
optimism, 118
ostrich, 42

painting, 2, 40
palm, 24
paper, 5
Parmenides, 37
parrots, 19
particle, 36, 134
pedantry, 126
penalty of failure, 53
pencil, 144
pencils, 5
pension, 112
perfection, 60, 130
pervert, 138
pessimism, 118
philosopher, 2, 3, 15, 18, 46, 64, 87, 114, 134, 137, 140
philosophers, 7, 12, 24, 116, 140
Philosophers' Stone, 86
philosophers, French, 4
philosophers, would-be, 15
philosophical logic, 117
philosophical systems, 76
philosophical temperament, 7, 46
philosophizing, 118
Philosophos, 75

philosophy, 1, 2, 13, 20, 25, 58, 65, 111, 114, 116, 131, 136
philosophy of mind, 79
philosophy of science, 141
physicists, 141, 142
physics, 46, 60, 95, 109, 142
physics, theoretical, 16
pigeon, 3
Plato, 40, 56, 99, 116, 119, 136, 143
Platonist, 119
Platonists, 13
plausible considerations, 126
plumbing, 50
poet, 130
poetry, 2, 40, 64, 134
police, 62
politician, 132
politicians, 83
politics, 2, 5, 132
porcelain, 2
possibilities, 19
possible worlds, 138
posterity, 7
potato, 4
practice, 136
pragmatist, 104
precise, 118
Presence, 37
Pressing Done Here, 76
priest, 34
primitivism, 52
principium cognoscendi, 43
principium essendi, 43
probabilities, 47
Professor Dennett, 31
professors, 134
propaganda, 92
protozoon, 117

pseudo problems, 25
psychiatry, 26

quack, 90
qualitative states, 15
quantum mechanics, 144
quantum theory, 60
quoit, 4

race, 146
rationality, 55
realism, 117, 142
Reality, 76
reason, 16, 73, 87
reciprocity, 139
'recognition', 70
references, 111
reflection, 107
relativism, 76
religion, 7, 64, 135
religious faith, 11
religious man, 34
reporter, 134
restaurant, 105
reverence, 91
reward of success, 53
rhetorics, 7
Ricky Martin, 29
rigour, 39
Roman empire, 88
Rome, 88
'ruminants', 96
Russell, 116

salvation, 5
Sartre, 52
scepticism, 122
scholar, 32
scholaticism, 113
science, 4, 5, 40, 44, 55, 57, 69, 70, 92, 111

science-fiction, 5, 31
scientific knowledge, 126
scientific philosophy, 44
scientist, 28, 57
scientists, 121, 142
Scottish school, 88
seduce, 123
selfishness, 49
sentiment, 64
sets, 46
sexual love, 87
shack, 76
shadow, 119
Sheehan, 37
shepherd, 125
shoddiness, 50
shooting, 9
shovel, 3
silliness, 145
skeptic, 126
skepticism, 40, 46, 52, 81
'slapdash egoism', 85
slavery, 136
slavish physicians, 19
society, 50
sociology, 107
Socrates, 28, 71
soldier, 134
solipsism, 45, 135, 144
solipsist, 119, 135
sophistry, 65
soul, 26
sound, 3
soya beans, 130
species, 8
spectacle, 87
spiders, 8
Spinoza, 44
spiritless, 147
spray gun, 25

square, 86
stable, 53
statuary, 2
Stoics, 108
stomach, 103, 125
stone, 91
struggles, 11
stupendous, 87
stupid, 118
style, 129
Substance, 29, 44
suicide, 23, 40
sunrise, 87
superstition, 126
Sustain, 41
symbols, 118
sympathy, 139

tapestry, 2
taste, 64, 131
tautology, 4
tea, 134
temperament, 131
Temple of Science, 10
terminology, 100
terms, 111
the human condition, 145
'the scientific method', 17
The Sleeper Spy, 61
Theologos, 75
theology, 75
theorist, quantum, 143
Thomas Aquinas, 101
time machines, 31
toilet, 26
toothache, 125
toper, 73
torch, 56, 121
traffic, 42
triangle, 86

trigger, 114
triumph, 121
truth, 7, 13, 28, 39, 56, 60, 65, 103, 115, 118, 135, 137, 141
truths, 5

Uncle Kant, 116
undertakers, 109
universals, 8
Universe, 1
universe, 70, 100
university education, 126

vague, 113, 118
vain, 2
values, 112
vanity, 11
variable, 111
variables, 112
Voltaire, 4
von Leipzig, 45

war, 2
weakness, 41
weight, 80
whisky, 35
William Saffire, 61
wisdom, 28, 97, 116, 136
Wittgenstein, 57
woman, 14, 86
women, 39, 134
wonder, 142
wooliness, 113
world, 118

yokel, 140
youth, 59

www.ingramcontent.com/pod-product-compliance
Lightning Source LLC
Chambersburg PA
CBHW021841220426
43663CB00005B/355